Praise For

HOW TO CHANGE A LAW

"The United States Supreme Court has acknowledged that lobbying elected officials in our democracy is 'among the most precious of the liberties safeguarded by the Bill of Rights, and intimately connected, both in origin and in purpose, with the other First Amendment rights of free speech and free press.'

"How to Change a Law" provides step-by-step, insider knowledge about how to enact or amend a statute. Everyone is frustrated with the level of inaction in Congress and our state legislatures. Now you can do something about it."

Steve Churchwell
Churchwell White LLP, and former General Counsel,
California Fair Political Practices Commission

"You can make a difference in your community. With this book you can actually create laws in your city, county or state. If you see things that need to change, buy this book and make it happen."

Robert A. Schuller
New York Times best-selling author, Walking In Your Own Shoes

"I've been a fan of John's for years now and 'H   ⁊ Law' does not disappoint. As Mayor of the Town   ᵗa, John's insights into the political process ar   .mpower people is real. If you're a concerr   .ap to create new policy ideas and solve som   .₃ as an advocate for a cause, this is for you."

Elizabeth Lewis
Mayor of Atherton

i

"I found this book to be an extremely useful --and almost DIY -- approach to taking back control of the elective process, and overcoming the sense that even an intelligent and well-intentioned individual can't really make a difference in today's political process. Mr. Thibault brings a beautiful knack for extracting the essential steps and approaches that can allow each of us to become empowered and re-energized in taking back politics from special interests, big business and highly paid lobbyists.

The whole concept of an I-lobby -- an individual process that anyone can utilize -- is an incredibly important contribution to today's political and cultural eco-system. An excellent contribution to our understanding of politics and the real workings of government -- and highly recommended."

Kevin O'Malley
President, TechTalk / Studio
Chairman, Business and Leadership Forum,
Commonwealth Club of California

"I have been deeply interested in politics and the political process my entire life, but it never even occurred to me that an average citizen could have any influence on the laws. A book like this is an act of optimism, because in the cynical age we live in, it takes a voice as passionate and persuasive as John Thibault's to mount the argument that if you really believe in something, you can actually start the wheels turning to make a difference.

John's book, and iLobby itself, are both constructive tools offered to citizens who, until now, didn't know they could be change-makers in a democracy which benefits from their participation and engagement in an age where apathy is, in most cases, the status quo."

Tim Knight
Founder, Prophet.Net
Author of Panic, Prosperity, and Progress

"This is one of the most important books written on the legislative process and how to participate in it. It is well-written and well-researched, so much so that I think the book should be part of the required curriculum for government classes at the high school and college level."

Gerri Knilans
President, Trade Press Services

"If you're anything like me, at numerous times throughout your life you've been frustrated by a law that just doesn't make sense. For 99% of people that's where the story ends. The challenges involved in understanding the process of effecting laws are daunting to most. Hopefully this book illustrates that challenging / changing a law is actually practical endeavor.

John Thibault's "How to Change a Law" is the first book that simplifies and literally lays out a blueprint on how to effectively have an impact on government and get things done. A first of it's kind in terms of simplicity and directness to how to actually be impactful in getting government to work for you."

Rob Smith
CEO, Pecabu

"It's incredibly refreshing to read a book like this one, where the reader is given tools to really help change our country. This isn't fluff; Thibault's strategies and system makes it doable for any person to affect our laws and make the changes we need going forward. How to Change a Law should be taught in our high schools, empowering not just our younger generation of change-makers but also educating them on our politics and government that are often overlooked or misunderstood. An easy read with actionable take-aways."

Gretchen Breuner
Author, The RoadScholarz

HOW TO
CHANGE
A

LAW

THE INTELLIGENT CONSUMER'S
7-STEP GUIDE

IMPROVE YOUR COMMUNITY,
INFLUENCE
YOUR COUNTRY, AND IMPACT THE
WORLD.

JOHN THIBAULT

iLobby LLC
325 Sharon Park Drive, #210
Menlo Park, CA 94025
www.ilobby.co

Disclaimer

This book is for educational purposes only and does not constitute an alternative to legal or other professional services advice. The publisher and author make no representations or warranties with respect to the accuracy or completeness of the contents of this book and disclaim any liability to any party with respect to any loss, damage, or disruption caused, or alleged to have been caused, by errors, omissions, information or programs contained herein. Any resemblance to actual persons, either living or dead, businesses, companies, events, or locales is coincidental. References are provided for informational purposes only and do not constitute endorsement of any websites or other sources.

Please watch this YouTube video.

https://www.youtube.com/watch?v=2FW8YTlZnqw

Visit Facebook Fan Page
http://www.facebook.com/ChangeALaw

Table of Contents

Acknowledgments

I want to thank my wife and close friends who encouraged me to take this to the next level and write this book. I also want to thank my editor for painstakingly going through the manuscript and making it more readable. I want to acknowledge the work of Napoleon Hill, Tony Robbins, Peter Diamandis and Brendon Burchard, who in a virtual way through books, videos and live events explained that there is a way to get information out there so we can lift our voices, and share our passions with a world that is desperately in need of better policy solutions.

PREFACE

Changing the law is hard work. It's not an easy thing to do. If you want to change a law you can either change the politicians or you can change the policy. This book is about changing policy.

Even though changing a law is hard I want to believe we can make the process simple, accessible and affordable so that you can participate. I wrote this book so that you can begin to improve your community, influence your leaders and impact the world.

I was interested in why so many of us, including myself, are frustrated by politics. I started my company, iLobby, with the belief that if people have access to a simpler yet more sophisticated way of changing laws, then this knowledge would relieve you of your frustration and allow you to take action.

What I'm trying to do is help you change your perspective so that you can be one of the few people in charge of your own political destiny.

That's it.

The people who are already familiar with government affairs "*get it*" and are well served by it. But for most Americans understanding what policy change is really about, was outside of their reach until now.

The information in this book should be freely available to as many people as possible so that voters like you can get things done. We can no longer afford to sit on the sidelines. You often hear people say, "It's time to take action...you've got to do this... elect a new leader, call your congressman..." but in reality it seems there's very little you can do to change outcomes for the better.

I hope this book helps you start thinking about a new way to reduce your political anxiety, get some relief from the frustration you might be feeling, and show you actual steps that you can take right now. Let me give you an example.

One way to think about this concept is relating it to baking a cake. You need a recipe with step-by-step instructions and specific quantities of ingredients to make a tasty, edible cake. If you follow the procedure correctly, then everyone will be satisfied with the outcome. However, if you mix up the ingredients or miss a step even your kids will think that your best baking is tasteless.

It is the same thing with political persuasion. There are a series of steps that need to be followed in a certain order. Protocol is essential and the strange thing about it is that it works. It's like political choreography and orchestration. When members of an orchestra playing different instruments come together and support a dramatic play or dance on stage the results can be stunning.

By the time you finish this book you will understand why you need a coherent message, why the players need to be orchestrated, sequenced and choreographed and why you need to put on the best performance of your life. This is the power of lobbying.

It's political theater at its best. Political choreography isn't just a science. It's an art form practiced by some of the most skilled political persuaders in the country.

If you ever expect the political machine to work, your schedule and choreography have to match with the politicians'. When you look at the US budget, it is a $3.8 trillion annual art form. And for the 212 million eligible voters in this country, it is costing each of us about $17,924 a year.

Countless people want to do "good" but what you don't realize is that in order to "do good" you may need to change a law.

In a clear and simple way, I will show you how to do this.

INTRODUCTION

Average Americans no longer trust the government. We have lost confidence in our leaders' ability to govern. Voters feel like they don't have a voice. They are frustrated, beaten-down and apathetic.

At the same time politicians are overwhelmed by the deluge and complexity of the problems they face. They want honest input from the voters in their district but they often don't get it. The promise of the Internet was that it would help us. But knowledge is doubling every 12 months and the pace has now overwhelmed Congress and our political leaders at every level of government.

Things are changing fast. The world is shifting and we have to try a new approach. We have to come together around issues, focus on new solutions and if we are serious and committed, put our money where our mouth is. We have to commit to taking control of our shared political destiny.

In this new approach the people who win will speak up and advocate for rational solutions. But the people who lose will be those who are distracted, who remain silent or who don't take any action at all.

The people who win will be those who want to help make the world a better place. The people who lose will be those who selfishly pursue their own self-interest at the expense of others.

We will call the people who win, "*Citizen Legislators*." The people who lose will not even be in the room.

How did I figure this out?

Throughout my career I, like many of us, didn't care about politics because I thought it didn't affect me. Then I met very successful people who were solving complex problems, and I realized that by modeling what they did anyone could do it too.

These were average people from every walk of life who set aside their differences and came together around issues, built coalitions, funded their initiatives and intelligently pursued their agenda.

But as I mentioned, the world is rapidly changing and what we need now is a place for the average person to also do this.

We need a platform that is affordable, independent, unbiased, nonpartisan, and issue-agnostic so that anyone can participate in it.

We need a *"Political Persuasion Platform™"* that empowers individuals to change laws. I call this *"crowd funded lobbying."*

That's what I am going to talk about in this book.

This book will give you a step-by-step guide. I will provide you with a map to this new territory, an overview so you know where you stand and where you're going. This book will empower you to go on this journey with others and me.

What I am about to tell you is not a secret, but less than 1% of the population understands it and uses it.

The information is out there. But it is complex, fragmented and confusing. Worse, most of us have misunderstandings about how the political persuasion process works. We have self-doubt, misinformation and myths that we need to overcome about our right to lobby and petition the government.

If you are frustrated by politics and politicians, maybe it's time you try something new. Something that is simple, understandable and manageable.

Although this framework is relatively simple, putting it all together can be challenging.

By design, this book is a companion to our website, iLobby located at https://www.ilobby.co

The iLobby Policy Framework (IPF) has three components:
1. Message
2. Mass
3. Money

The purpose of this book is to give you some insight, actionable tools and strategies that you can implement on "Day One."

I want to help you move from being a frustrated voter who is disgusted with the system to a more engaged citizen who realizes that your participation in public policy truly matters.

I will show you why a clear, specific message is so important. We will talk about why you need a large enough mass of people who believe and support you in what you're doing in order to succeed. And we will talk about why money and resources are essential to helping you sustain your effort.

We are at a turning point where you need to get involved in setting policy. Policy discussions lead to laws. Laws enable decisions. Decisions lead to action and solutions to our global problems.

Before you begin on any journey though, you need a map. This book will give you a bird's eye view of the territory.

I will talk about what roadblocks you might encounter, what policy success looks like, some of the common myths we have and mistakes that we make. And what's in it for you.

You will learn to vote on issues, not for candidates. Most of us confuse politics with policy. So let me clear the air. In this book we're <u>not</u> talking about getting people elected to office. We are talking about helping our elected leaders find solutions to problems that affect all of us. Issues like student debt, gun violence, immigration, cyber security, privacy, ISIS, energy independence, healthcare, taxes etc.

If you are willing to go on the journey with me, you will be on the road to becoming a *"Citizen Legislator."*

If you are concerned about where the country is going, then this book is for you. If you are fed up with government incompetence, then this book is for you. If you believe deep down that you have something to offer, then this book is for you.

How to Change a Law will give you insights, tools and the map that you need to make change happen.

So let's get started!

John Thibault
Founder, CEO iLobby

Chapter 1

WHAT THIS BOOK CAN DO FOR YOU

~ STEP 1 ~
Time required: 4 minutes

~ DAY 1 ~
Sign up at iLobby (https://www.ilobby.co)
Find a debate, any debate and vote on it.

> "Let us never forget that government is ourselves
> and not an alien power over us. The ultimate rulers
> of our democracy are not a President and senators and
> congressmen and government officials, but the
> voters of this country."
>
> ~Franklin D. Roosevelt~

My Promise to You

If you have ever wanted to change a law, then this book will show you how. If you have ever thought a law was unjust or unfair, then this book will show you a new approach to changing laws. If you ever felt confused and frustrated by bureaucracy, then this book will show you how to navigate through the government channels.

Affecting legislation is all about persuasion. And persuasion in the field of government relations, is called lobbying. Hopefully by the end of this book you will see that lobbying is not the enemy. Lobbying is one of the most important tools you can lawfully use to advocate for change.

In the United States, the First Amendment of the Bill of Rights grants citizens the right to petition the government and is thus a constitutionally guaranteed right. This right has been around since our founding and the top 1% of the population use it consistently to achieve the laws, rules and regulations that they want. Now it's time for you to join them.

Maybe one of the reasons you do not engage is because of the complexity involved. I hope to take what is inherently complex and make it simple and understandable. But more importantly, actionable. Maybe one of the reasons you do not engage is because you focus on politics and not policy. I will distinguish between the two, and show you that electioneering and candidates are different from issues. The issues are what we want to focus on here.

Maybe you choose not to engage because you perceive lobbying as too expensive. And therefore you simply cannot afford it. I will show you how crowd funded lobbying can level the playing field and how you too, can enter the game.

If you think the voice of the voter should finally be heard, then this book is for you. If you are committed and follow the strategy that I will teach you, then, together we will demystify politics. I will help you understand why politics is so complex and why it's so hard to get anything done. I will show you an actionable

8

framework and method that top advocates use successfully every day.

It essentially requires three things; (1) Message, (2) Mass and (3) Money.

I will show you why a clear, specific message (a common methodical approach, point of view and position) is important. We will talk about why you need a large enough mass (group, coalition) of voters who believe in what you're doing in order to succeed and finally we will talk about why capital, resources and commitment are essential to sustaining your efforts.

Because without clear communications, committed constituents and sufficient capital, you will not be able to have an effect on policy and you will not be able to change the law.

Hopefully, we will do away with the civics lessons and the arcane language. Let's see if we can demystify public policy and simplify, simplify, simplify.

Simple does not equal easy

One more caveat. This book is about solving problems for many people, not just one person.

I am not an ombudsman. At iLobby, we do not fix traffic tickets or appeal to Government departments for your personal benefit or to get individual economic relief. This is not about seeking remedies within the judicial system. We do not advocate signing petitions with the executive branch. We are focused on the legislative branch and to a lesser extent will talk about the agencies.

Though this book may seem narrowly focused, it is intended to be practical and to be used as a proactive tool. Legislators are in office because we voted them into office. It is their job to listen to their constituents. That's all of us. We would like to help you amplify your voice and have thus created a collaborative, communications platform between you, the voter, and your elected leader.

We have bridged the gap by introducing one new element; a professional government affairs person to intercede on your behalf.

Welcome to Lobbying 101. I want to caution you that there are many ways to go astray. We'll talk about that too.

By knowing and avoiding the pitfalls and focusing on what you hope to accomplish, perhaps this book can reduce some of the frustration you feel and put you on the path to solving problems in your community.

You might think the idea of distinguishing between politics and policy doesn't matter. But it does. Some people say you should leave this to the experts because average people can't possibly understand public policy.

We have already tried that. Let's learn from the results. Doubters might say that you should not be engaged in policy because you don't have the ability to actually get anything done. In chapter 5 I will show you the case of a 10-year-old girl getting a law passed.

We know some government experts and even politicians do not trust the wisdom of the crowd. However when considering our education and technological future, I think this is shortsighted. It is extremely harmful to the economy, the country and our well-being when the government does not want to hear from or involve the people.

We are at a turning point in this country. You need to step up and get involved in setting policy because policy solves problems and leads to laws. Voting on issues and laws enables decision-making. Decisions lead to actions that affect all of us.

So think of this as a journey. It's not a sprint. It's a marathon. You need to learn, take a course, train and compete. You need to be in shape. You need a coach, a team, and a strategy. You need to know what you're getting into.

There are people who are changing laws now, thousands of them every single day. They know how to work through the process. After a little guidance, you can be one of those people too.

You've waited long enough.

This book will finally give you the tools needed to move from living a couch potato lifestyle to becoming an involved and knowledgeable citizen, maybe even an activist. You have to admit, it's a step in the right direction, even if you are still sitting down.

So let's first learn how to get organized, how to influence others, and how to convince people to support you. And we will learn how to convince your leaders to implement your great ideas.

Your efforts, even your best efforts, won't work every time. But by engaging fully in the persuasion/sales/lobbying process, you will strip away the non-essentials. We will help you focus on key activities you need to do to get something done.

America is frustrated with its leaders. Over 80% of the population thinks Congress isn't doing their job. Yet we still elect the same people over and over again.

The information you'll find here is available to the public. But you really have to dig for it. I have already done this for you. If you've tried everything else, then try this and see what happens.

For some of you, the information you read here might seem oversimplified. For others, this may be your first introduction to the world of Government affairs when it comes to persuading or lobbying for truly representative legislation.

If you are eager to skip ahead you can go directly to Chapter 7, the iLobby solution.

I will show you a new way of thinking and a step-by-step approach to changing a law.

So… what will you learn?

You'll learn how to discover issues you're concerned about, share them with like-minded people, and build a stellar case for the law you want to support. You'll learn to transform your frustration into action, your apathy into intention. You'll develop an increased sense of hope for our country and trust in your government again.

I know this is an optimistic approach, but I believe it will work.

Best of all, you'll have a better understanding of how things actually work so that you can make the changes you so desperately want to see.

That's my promise to you.

Chapter 2

WHAT'S IN IT FOR ME?

~ STEP 2 ~

Time required: 3 minutes

~ DAY 2 ~

Find another debate, any debate. Read the comments and arguments and then vote on it.

> *"The heaviest penalty for declining to rule is to be ruled by someone inferior to yourself."*
>
> **~Plato, The Republic~**

Who should read this book?

Who is this book for?

Concerned citizens like you and me, people who care about the future of the country; the inquisitive, the disgruntled, those with some intellectual curiosity. This is for anyone who wants to help his or her neighbor or really wants to make a difference in the world.

If you're happy about how things are going politically and you're not interested in learning, then this book is definitely NOT for you.

There are 196 countries in the world. There are 123 democracies. Of these there are approximately 25 first world countries. This book is intended for those who are looking for peaceful, rational solutions to complex problems no matter the size or scale.

Politics is everyone's "third" favorite hobby.

Benefits of effective persuasion/sales

There are four kinds of people who can benefit from this book:

- Voters
- Small businesses
- Lobbyists
- Politicians

Policy and laws affect all of us and each of these groups in someway defines policy and the laws we live by.

For Voters

I can help you see how changing a law can be simple, easier, more convenient and more affordable than you think.

Most voters believe it's hard to be heard above the noise. So they do nothing. But by joining in a debate, you can propose a new law or change an existing law. When you've learned the ropes and know how persuasion works, nothing is impossible.

You'll feel empowered to participate. You'll be more engaged and better understand policy, so you'll be less frustrated and more educated about the political messages you're hearing and delivering.

My hope is that you'll connect with other like-minded people who are as eager as you are to make the changes that you want to see in the world.

For Small Business

Small businesses can benefit through increased issue control, saved time and saved money.

Whether you're a member of a small business association or your industry wants to push forward a ballot measure in your state, effective persuasion gives any small business the chance to clarify its message and connect with other like-minded businesses and their employees.

Because it's your agenda, you initiate the issues that are most important to you. You don't have to leave it to your trade association. They may not think your local issue is worth presenting to a larger audience. This book puts the power and control back in your hands—where it belongs.

For Lobbyists

Lobbyists educate their clients about the legislative process. They then inform lawmakers about their clients' interests. In fact, that's often how they spend most of their time. You might be under the mistaken belief that lobbyists can change a law with the snap of their fingers. But that's just not true.

By taking on more informed clients at an earlier stage, you as a lobbyist can accelerate the pace, get more informed clients and have a bigger impact with constituent advocacy.

Share this book with your clients. It's a way to help them sharpen their arguments and build a larger grassroots following, even before they start working with you. It can be a smoother onramp as you help make their case stronger and your job easier.

For Politicians

Politicians are always looking for feedback from their constituents. As a politician maybe you have come to rely on surveys and polls to gain insight because you find it difficult to consistently reach your voters. However, as you know, one-to-one communication is central to your ability to accurately represent your constituents.

When you host a Town hall meeting, do enough people show up? Often not. Now you can take some of the key issues where you want constituent input and make them available online. This will make it easier for your constituents to give feedback or perhaps support a potential piece of legislation that you're considering.

For those in your district who cannot be present at meetings, this book and the iLobby platform will give them the opportunity to provide input in a simple, effective way. Viewing constituents' positions on the platform is straightforward because the arguments are organized and separated at the outset.

In the end, you'll be able to compose and deliver a clear message and craft better legislation with your staff and other stakeholders. You won't need to rely solely on "special interests." You'll know that your constituents are informed well before a final vote. You'll know whether or not your voters support you and you'll get an idea of how many of them are equally committed to following through and "making it so".

How you can benefit

To make this work, you'll need a sense of purpose and you'll need to follow your passion. You have to be willing to contribute to something greater than yourself. You have to be committed.

This is why a single vote counts. This is why a single comment or share makes a difference. Because when you combine your small efforts with millions of other people's efforts, you can change a law.

You aren't alone. You just haven't found the proper place to express your passion for policy yet!

You have to engage for the sake of engagement, because you know it's the right thing to do. You have to pick the issues that you care most about and be willing to do whatever it takes to move them forward legally, rationally, and with the help of your neighbors, your community, and your elected representatives. This is the secret to changing a law.

Believing in yourself is necessary. You need to do the things that matter to you. You need to believe that you can attract the people and the resources you'll need. You'll need to believe that what you do will impact core beliefs, which are essential to making a difference in the world.

Your job here on earth is bigger than you ever imagined. Your thoughts, ideas and approaches can benefit thousands, perhaps even millions of people. It is your higher purpose that will sustain you through the tough times and opposition you'll face as you move forward.

So let's start exploring the pathway to political lobbying mastery.

What's in it for me?

"Why should I do this? Why should I take on this huge project only to see so little return? It's too ephemeral. It's not tangible. There's no immediate gratification."

Clearly, a person who thinks this way isn't going to become an advocate for a cause bigger than himself or herself. It isn't in their DNA.

What we are doing is non-obvious. That's why so few people do it. Unlike a traditional offer that you might hear on the radio or read in a newspaper ad where you give them your credit card and they send you a product, we are not asking you to give us your money. Nor are we sending you a product. So this does not offer a tangible and immediate gratification. This is non-tangible and delayed. And that's why it's not obvious. That's why only intelligent consumers actually ever do it.

Lobbying is a non-obvious, long-term solution to political frustration, apathy and ennui. It offers no guarantee but when it works and is done right, the results can be incredible and gratifying on a higher order. But the success affords benefit to the whole group, your community, and your nation, not just one individual. It helps society.

And that's why it's *not* obvious.

Does this mean that every individual who takes on the challenge of changing a law is doing it for selfless reasons? Not at all.

But I think they envision a greater good for their community and their world. They know that ultimately, there will be social benefit, some value in return. They gain the benefit, personal recognition, and earn the reputation of someone who is an influencer, a leader, someone who has taken on a tough challenge and contributed to a great effort.

It is this set of nobler values that I believe leads people to take on the challenge of doing good work in the world and in their community and trying to set things right. People do this through volunteer work, helping others, teaching, public service etc.

It doesn't have to take up all of your time. But if you've ever volunteered in a soup kitchen, or helped out with a youth group or acted as a mentor for the younger generation, all of this would have helped. If you were ever involved in relief efforts after storm damage here in our country or in other parts of the world, you know the emotional benefit you receive by engaging with the community, reaching out, and giving people a helping hand. Your self-esteem shoots up and you realize there's a transcendent value in helping others.

The same thing applies here. In some cases, you'll reap an economic benefit. But as a group, you can make a significant impact and everyone will participate in the benefits.

Changing the law shouldn't be something that is hard to do. But it is hard, done infrequently, or done with a grudge.

When you use crowd funded lobbying, you're not going to get a T-shirt.

For some reason there's something inside each of us that is always looking to improve things. A lot of people tinker with things, make things, and create things. We encourage people to play around, test ideas, test a hypothesis, and try new things. It's fun to solve problems.

Kids in middle school are now expected to advocate for themselves even if they don't yet know what "advocate" means. At an early age, kids are learning to program. Computers make it easy to for people to revise code, essays and ideas, to create wikis, and to collaborate and work in groups. In Silicon Valley we encourage failure and learning. Some of our biggest failures and tinkering have turned into major companies and industries.

So what if this intellectual curiosity were applied to laws?

These days you contribute to the world in larger ways than you were able to as a dependent child. You make and prescribe positive changes. You shape your community, your company, and your industry. You set policy. ('Policy' is your way of providing guidance for other people by writing it down and turning it into a law.) You're putting your fingerprint on the world. You're showing that you're here and can make a difference.

Isn't that what everyone wants to do?

You're not destroying things; you're not tearing things down. You're not crying out for someone else to solve your problems. You're saying, "I have a point of view. I can influence others and encourage them to work with me. I feel good about exploring and tackling big challenges."

Yes… and ultimately making that legacy-making difference.

Why this is important?

So, here are 50 reasons why you might consider doing this.

50 Reasons Why You Should Do This

1. You will feel gratified
2. You will help others
3. You will make friends you never imagined possible
4. You will build a community of meaningful relationships
5. You will make a difference
6. You will become an expert
7. You will step up
8. You will contribute to a cause bigger than yourself
9. You will shape the future of others
10. You will affect your destiny
11. You will have fun
12. You can take on and master a complex challenge
13. You will get to express yourself
14. Your point of view is important
15. It doesn't take a lot of time, money or resources
16. What you have to say matters
17. You are a force to be reckoned with
18. You are part of the human race
19. You will make things happen
20. You might save a life
21. You could prevent harm
22. You could save an industry
23. You may promote small business interests
24. You are on the ground floor of a movement
25. You will feel pride of authorship
26. You will get your name out there
27. You will become significant
28. You are acknowledged by the media as an expert
29. You will have an adventure
30. You will change the world

31. You receive positive peer review for your excellent contributions to public policy
32. You take on a challenge
33. You could write a book or a magazine article about your personal experiences
34. You can get a law named after yourself
35. You will meet new people you have great respect for
36. You will no longer hide in the shadows
37. You could become famous
38. You might be interviewed
39. You could save a tremendous amount of time
40. You might save some money or actually make some money
41. You want to start a movement
42. You could become a confidante and an influencer of your elected leaders
43. You might be inspired to run for public office
44. You might realize someone you know would be a great politician
45. You will improve your community
46. You will influence your leaders
47. You will impact the world
48. You will improve your self-esteem
49. You will define the future in key areas like space, medicine, robotics, technology, energy, defense, education and healthcare
50. People and countries less fortunate than you are counting on you

Do you need more reasons?

Chapter 3

NO ONE SAID ANYTHING ABOUT DETOURS

~ STEP 3 ~

Time required: 10 minutes

~ DAY 3 ~

Pick a debate, any debate and add
a short argument of your own, pro or con.

"The ultimate measure of a man is not where he stands in moments of comfort and convenience, but where he stands at times of challenge and controversy."

~Martin Luther King, Jr. ~

Imagine you are driving down the freeway on a clear, sunny day. The ride is smooth, fast and enjoyable. Then you get off at an exit and proceed down a two lane highway that leads to a narrow and bumpy gravel road.

After a few miles of this you are forced to slow down. You discover a fallen tree up ahead blocking your route. You are forced to turn around and try another road. The detour takes you out of your way and onto a forest service road.

It's getting dark. You've wasted a lot of time. It starts to rain and now you're running out of gas. You check your phone. You have no cell service. You are in the middle of nowhere. You're tired, lost and alone.

But it gets worse. It's now nighttime and it's raining hard. The car is making a funny sound. Then you have a blowout. You stop; pop open the trunk and check your spare tire. It's flat. You remember that you never replaced it from the last time you had a blowout. You just forgot. You are frustrated, hungry, lost, cold, confused and in the dark.

If this picture sounds bleak, it is.

Welcome to American politics.

You often hear people say things like.

"It's hard to be heard."
"It's difficult to know what to say."
"It's complicated."
"The game is rigged."
"My voice doesn't matter."
"An individual can't do anything anyway."

Sound familiar?

100 years ago Henry Ford invented the Model T automobile to provide *"affordable transportation"* to everyone. Though it wasn't perfect at first, his car began to transform the American

landscape. It provided mobility, opportunity and freedom to the masses; but not without a few bumps and mishaps along the way.

Through the knowledge you will gain in this book I want to provide you with the opportunity to obtain *affordable lobbying* so you will never be lost again.

I will show you that there is a way to get past the roadblocks.

Roadblocks

There are two kinds of roadblocks to your advocacy success, internal and external

I have grouped the internal roadblocks as follows:
- Self-doubt
- Ignorance
- Apathy

The external roadblocks are:
- Time
- Money
- Resources
- Tactics

Whether you call these detours or roadblocks, in every case they slow you down or take you down the wrong road.

Self-doubt

We have self-doubt because we confuse politics with policy. When we are confused we tend to stop and do not take action. It's because we have conflicting information.

Politics is about elections. Policy, as I define it, is about issues.

You also might have self-doubt because you believe that you have to come up with the whole solution. You don't. That's why we use crowd sourcing. This is like a puzzle. You may have one piece of the puzzle and somebody else will have a different piece.

If you've ever been to a football game and seen fans holding up individual letters that create an exciting message for the opposing enthusiasts on the other side of the stadium, then you'll know what I'm talking about. As individuals they do not understand their own personal contribution. They hold up one letter. It seems meaningless. But choreographed in unison the letters come together in a specific way that is incredibly powerful. Each individual person plays a very small part, but altogether they make a huge impact.

Complexity also enters the picture because the language of issues and bills has become so elevated that it excludes anyone but the most trained legal minds. However, before the words turn into legalese, ideas are usually discussed in general, colloquial, everyday terms.

Ignorance

If you do not have a critical thinking mindset or if you are simply relying on one source of information, you are doing yourself a disservice. By not getting all the facts, you are keeping yourself in a state of low information and you're not aware of all sides of an issue.

This is not necessarily your fault.

I touched on this earlier but you need to be aware of it. Some people jump to the conclusion that when they talk about politics, they think it only has to do with the candidates running for elected office. So I want to distinguish here that we are talking about policy.

Think about this.

After you elect somebody into office, what do they talk about? Issues. That's what voters keep bringing up. They want to know what the politician's position is on an issue and they want to see if that issue and position matches up with their own ideology.

Because we are focused on issues at iLobby, we are not concerned with political parties. Most issues are not consigned to a single party anyway. Think about it. Is education a Democrat or Republican issue? Are taxes Democrat or Republican? Is defense

Republican or Democrat? Either or both. What distinguishes the party platform is the *position* each party takes on a particular issue.

But the difficulty is that the parties only advocate for their side and they don't give you all the facts about the opposition. Now that you understand this, you are in a better position to decide for yourself.

Apathy

If you don't care about issues then it's probably because you are disconnected from the real events or the outcome. You might feel powerless to do anything. You mistakenly believe that in order to be effective you have to do a massive amount of work, and that simply is not true.

When you put these three things together, self-doubt, ignorance and apathy, and additionally you don't believe in yourself, don't have any ideas, and are not dissatisfied enough to get the real facts, you are at an incredible disadvantage. This is because there are other people who will prevail and generally will do so at your expense.

Now, let's take a look at the external obstacles you face.

Time

You do not believe that you have the time to think about public policy. In the old way of doing things, it took a huge amount of time to get up to speed and to get anything done. That is no longer the case. Maybe you do not think you have the luxury of time. Maybe you think that you can't afford to take the time required to focus on issues.

But if you look around your neighborhood, your workplace or the country you will see that we are surrounded by issues every day of the week. They exist in our community, in our state and at the federal level. If you share the burden of clarifying issues with other people this will take less of your time than you think. No one is asking you to drop everything and do the work by yourself. In our framework you work with other people at your convenience.

Money

You mistakenly believe that this is about giving money to politicians to run for election but I assure you, it is not. Do you think that it is expensive to have someone advocate on your behalf? Not anymore. First of all, you are not required to put any money into the game. Your ideas are more important than your cash. Your expertise and your opinion are more critical than your bank account.

But for those of you who do want to participate, you can pledge a small amount. The key is that you have to have enough people to play the game. Out of the population of 315 million people it is hard to believe that there are not 20,000 or 30,000 frustrated people who would easily give up one movie per year to get an issue or a bill moved into law.

It doesn't take as much as you think.

Resources

This is where most people go astray. They look at the choices available to them from the old way of doing things and think the old way is the only way that they can get legislative change. But this is not true.

Maybe you rely on calling talk radio, writing letters to your congressman, posting on a blog, protesting in the streets or signing a petition. I am not saying there's anything wrong with doing any of these things. In fact, if you're already doing them then I encourage you to continue.

However, I am just suggesting that many of these methods do not allow you to build a focused, effective, ad hoc coalition of like-minded people. So while these above efforts might seem like the right thing to do, they most likely will not lead you to legislative success. These actions are not as helpful as the new framework that we are talking about here with iLobby. There are other obstacles, roadblocks and detours that can derail your efforts but for now these are the top level ones that I want to bring to your attention.

Once you know about and understand them, you can plan a way to overcome them. You will then be in a much better position to take on the challenges associated with changing a law.

When you compare the methods of contact we currently have to get your message out, you can see which ones have a negative sign and may not be the best option for you.

Comparison of Advocacy Methods

	Message	Mass	Money
Letter/email	+	-	-
March/protest	-	+	-
Petition	+	+	-
Talk radio	+	-	-
Blog post	+	-	-
Town hall	+	+	-
Fly in	+	+	+
Lobbying	+	+	+

You might think that it is impossible to have an affect in Congress or your home state. But it's not. New laws and regulations are passed every day. They aren't passed by accident.

Someone moved them forward. Policy advocates don't always get what they want but they do get it often enough that this activity is worthwhile for them. They understand the roadblocks and they know how to navigate around them. Thus you need these experts in your corner.

Don't let the system stand in your way. You can get something done. If you apply the right methods and pull a team together to make it happen, you can resolve a complex issue and make a positive change.

But you have to be proactive. You can't have a defensive state of mind. You can't wait until the problem becomes so large that you become too despondent to do something about it. The time to take action is *before* the problem occurs.

The only solution is you

It's time for you to take a stand, make a decision, and do the right thing. It's time for you to step up, and be better than you have ever been before.

So get into the game early on while we're still in the pre-game, pre-legislative stage. In the next chapter I will show you how I learned about this and how you can too.

Chapter 4

THE POLITICAL GENE

~ STEP 4 ~

Time required: 9 minutes

~ DAY 4 ~

Browse through the issues. Then select a debate, any debate and pledge $50 of your virtual currency.

> *"Democracy is worth dying for, because it's the most deeply honourable form of government ever devised by man."*
>
> **~Ronald Reagan~**

Let me tell you how I arrived at the point where I learned that policy matters.

When I was a kid I picked up a bug at a summer fair. I was 11 years old. School started a few days later. At recess I was playing dodge ball with my friends at my elementary school when I felt hot, woozy and then collapsed on the school playground. The next thing I knew I was in the hospital. I stayed there for a week and no one could come to visit me. When they were finally ready to release me the doctor said to me that because of my illness, it was unlikely I would live past the age of 35.

I was shocked and scared but I didn't tell my parents what he said. So, every year from the age of 11 until I was 35 I was incredibly apprehensive thinking that I might die any day.

While other kids were planning what they would be when they grew up, I was too indecisive to commit to anything. I was unwilling to make plans for the future. Some people just thought I was shy and introverted. I was resigned, fatalistic and withdrawn.

I reasoned that if I didn't have a lot of time left in my life, then I should just follow my passions; follow my dreams. I was an average student. I skied in the winter. I played in a band. Then when I graduated high school I suddenly quit music, the thing that I enjoyed the most. My friends and band members never believed that I would give it up. But I did.

It was the late 60s and I was fascinated by television and the power of the media. When I turned 19, I moved away from home and told my roommate that I needed to document my life. I started to write an autobiography. I was only five pages into it when I realized that I was still too young. I hadn't lived and I really had nothing to say. I put my memoirs on the shelf for a while... a long while.

While my college friends were pursuing degrees in law, medicine, architecture, economics and business, I had a dream that somehow I had something to say. I had something to contribute to society. I didn't know what my message was and I didn't know how to get it out. But I knew telling *"my story"* wasn't the answer.

I was influenced by Marshall McLuhan who said, *"The medium is the message."* I knew I had to do something.

I focused on television and film and ultimately set my sights on Hollywood. It was a long journey to get there but eventually I was accepted into UCLA's graduate film school.

I felt like I blossomed there. From my mid 20s through my mid 30s I worked on crafting an inspirational message and trying to get it out to the world. I wanted to tell the story of other people. So I figured fiction was the way to do this. I aspired to learn how to write and direct movies. I dreamed that someday I would win an Academy award at the Oscars and then be able to give an inspirational three-minute speech to tens of millions of people around the world.

However, this wasn't just *my* dream. It was the dream of so many other creative people who were focused on industry success.

I wrote 21 screenplays, two novels and a book of poetry. I had an agent. Properties were optioned. There was interest off and on but somehow the stars did not align.

As I approached my 35th birthday I was becoming restless and very worried. Deep in my unconscious, I started to remember that my days were numbered. Death was right around the corner.

I can't tell you how relieved I was once that fateful day passed. The doctor was wrong. I wasn't dead. What a relief!

I enjoyed the next few days and weeks. I had a new lease on life. But then I thought, "Well, I'm here now. I've wasted all this time worrying about nothing. I really have to do something. What am I going to do?"

Getting my message out by trying to be a screenwriter and director wasn't working for me. I knew I had to make a change.

I was self-taught on computers and excited by technology. I had been consulting at the studios while writing at night and on weekends. Eventually through one of my assignments I ended up at the door of the parent company of Universal Studios, MCA. One particular assignment led to an opportunity at the corporate headquarters on the lot.

The folks seemed like really genuine people and after a week they offered me a full-time position. But it wasn't in film production or writing. It was in Government Relations.

Sometimes life throws us a curveball. We get an opportunity to do things that we are unqualified for, overqualified or something in between.

I knew I had a natural gift to get along with different kinds of people, a gift I didn't really recognize for a long time. I was also good at creating and resolving tension and conflict because that's what screenwriters do.

I was intellectually curious, interested in global affairs and the problems on the world stage.

So when they told me that this position in GR (Government relations) would allow me to interface with congressman and Senators in Washington, their staff, the administration, heads of state, civic leaders, state legislators and heads of studios, I was delighted.

I thought through these high-level contacts somehow this would be my big break. Finally, I would be able to sell a screenplay.

In reality, I received a firsthand lesson in political persuasion at the highest level.

Our small government affairs department reported directly to MCA's legendary Chairman, Lew Wasserman. For three intense years, I learned about issues, policy, FEC (Federal Election Commission) reporting, FPPC (Fair Political Practices Commission) compliance as it applied to our PAC (political action committee), working with lobbyists, fundraisers, electioneering, security details and protocol.

Of the political leaders we interfaced with at the time, many are household names and some are still in office.

Although I relished this exposure and had great access, I still had a nagging feeling that the thing I was supposed to do was yet to come. The stage I was supposed to be involved in had not yet been built. The technology I needed did not yet exist. My time had not come. A small voice inside me said I needed to wait longer.

Naturally, I did not want to wait any longer. But there was nothing I could do about it.

Then, in early April 1993 my father suddenly died. It was the first funeral I had ever attended in my life. As often happens with a family death, this set me back on my heels and my own mortality once again came back into focus.

I sensed a change on the horizon but I did not know what it was.

California was facing a wicked recession. The Rodney King riots had just taken place a year earlier. Graffiti started creeping onto the buildings in upscale Westwood. An innocent woman was attacked in broad daylight on Malibu Beach. This sort of thing just didn't happen along the tony greenbelt between Malibu and Beverly Hills. The level of increased violence in LA was palpable. Carjacking was becoming a common occurrence. A billboard popped up saying "The last one to leave California, please turn off the lights."

When we undergo change, there is often a buildup of tension that goes on for a very long time and then, *snap*, in an instant, an immediate release. When the release happens it can be jarring, revolutionary and destructive.

On the morning of Tuesday April 21, 1993 the MCA "Black Tower" came under sniper attack.

I was in my office on the fifth floor facing the street when I heard the first shots. Some of my coworkers on the floor explained it away as special effects on the back lot. But when high caliber bullets pierced the large glass panes of the building and penetrated through the walls, it was clear that this was not SFX.

I quickly got down on my hands and knees and crawled away from the windows. As I inched past cubicles, the sounds of bullets ricocheting in the elevator shaft made you think there were shooters arriving from every direction. No one knew where to go. There was no place to hide. The gunfire seemed to go on forever. At first a few of us ran toward the elevators thinking we would get out but when we heard the sound of gunfire inside the elevator shaft we abandoned that idea. Others tried the stairwell. But the barrage echoing in there was just as ominous. It seemed like there were two or three shooters. We were surrounded.

In moments like this you don't know if you will live or die. I thought to myself, "I live in a safe place and I work in a gated studio lot and still I was not safe."

I would never fulfill my mission. I would never discover my purpose in life. I would never be able to inspire others. In fact maybe that doctor from long ago was right. I would die young.

A few minutes later we heard the thundering roar of police helicopters overhead. The shooting continued. Then there was silence. We waited.

When the shooting stopped I was relieved. I patted myself to make sure I was in one piece. I walked around the floor and saw bullet holes the size of a half dollar in the walls. Like so many of my coworkers, I could say, "I am still here."

After a few more minutes the elevator doors opened and out walked chairman Lew Wasserman with a small security detail. He was going from floor to floor of the 15-story office tower to make sure that all his employees were safe. They were. Except for a few folks who heard the shots and by mistake went to the windows where they were wounded by flying glass.

Fortunately, no one was killed.

In the aftermath, we watched the events play out on television and in the press. My wife had seen the events immediately on local TV. She could not reach me and did not know if I was alive or dead.

Later, we learned that the shooter was a disgruntled former employee with a high-powered bolt-action Remington 700-BDL rifle with a telescopic sight. He sprayed a barrage of three dozen bullets from the 4th to the 14th floor. He had been let go 7 years earlier and he had never recovered from that. All that time he held a grudge against the vice president who he felt was responsible for his termination. And so now he felt justified in attempting to terminate the lives of others.

Sometimes pain and struggle comes in waves like the ocean, in sets of three. Sometimes it carries over time to larger intervals.

Nine months after the shooting the earth decided it too had built up enough tension and it was time for an immediate and unexpected release.

At 4:30 AM on January 17, 1994, the ground in Southern California snapped open along a previously unknown blind thrust fault erupting in a 6.7-magnitude quake that struck the San

Fernando Valley. It was referred to as the Northridge earthquake. The quake caused upwards of $20 billion in damages in less than 20 seconds and produced the fastest ground acceleration ever recorded in an urban area in North America.

At the time my wife and I owned a condominium in Calabasas, 13 miles from the Reseda epicenter. Thankfully, we were not there at the time but we later learned that the refrigerator literally flew across the kitchen. For others it was much worse. We also had the unpleasant shock of discovering that some of the units in our development had been red tagged, which meant they were uninhabitable.

The condominium residents believed that earthquake insurance would cover the loss. But it turned out that the property manager had stopped paying the insurance and instead had been embezzling homeowner association fees. All the owners would collectively bear the brunt of paying for the losses on all the damaged units. It was an unbelievable financial mess.

In spite of this and other difficulties, I still sensed that there was some new event waiting on the horizon. That trend turned out to be the rapid growth and deployment of the Internet throughout the 1990s.

When I determined that this could actually be the medium that Marshall McLuhan had referred to; that this might finally allow me to get my message out, I was thrilled. I felt like I was in my element, that I was riding a generational wave.

By late 1996 I joined a small Silicon Valley startup focused on online auctions; something I knew nothing about and that I was either overqualified or unqualified for or somewhere in between.

But that's another story.

The blending of Internet technology, influence and politics eventually led me to the creation of this book.

Finally, I felt like I had a clear idea of what my message was. I knew who the audience was and I knew that this was a shared, critical time for millions of us. People needed to know what I had learned in the corporate halls at MCA. Americans needed to understand what Washington insiders have taken for granted.

Voters needed to recognize that laws affect every aspect of our lives, that public policy matters!

Chapter 5

POLICY SUCCESS STORIES

~ **STEP 5** ~

Time required: 3 minutes

~ **DAY 5** ~

Pick a debate, any debate and share it
on your favorite social network.

---

*"The care of human life and happiness, and not
their destruction, is the first and only object
of good government."*

~Thomas Jefferson~

We recognize that there are many difficulties in getting a law passed. But it all starts with one individual. In the cases I am about to present, a person saw a problem and wanted to implement a solution. Sometimes the facts are compelling enough to convince others. In other cases it was a personal story.

What you'll see here are how clear, honest, compelling, authentic stories often win the day.

But, there has to be an advocate for a cause. Without one you won't succeed. Let's take a look at some winning examples.

Case #1 –
Mary's Neighborhood Trash Collection – Local Issue

A few years ago, our neighborhood trash service moved our pickup day from Thursday to Monday. Many of the residents were elderly. They had long driveways on flag lots. These are homes that are located 200 feet from the street behind the street facing homes. This made it difficult for them to roll the 200-pound trash bin to the street by themselves.

Also, the town had recently initiated a 24-hour ordinance about not leaving trash bins at the curb. Residents who put their trash bins out on Friday night worried that they would be cited for the 24-hour violation and have to pay a $100 fine.

A gardener would normally take their trash bins out for them on the appropriate weekday night. However the Monday garbage schedule change eliminated this helpful option because the gardeners do not work on Sundays.

A neighbor, I'll call her Mary, contacted the waste company to explain the situation but she got nowhere. They told her the change was now the new policy. When a company says this is our "policy" it usually stops any further dialogue right there. The routes had just been changed and they could not change them again. My neighbor escalated this to the manager and still got the same answer.

I spoke with Mary and suggested that the best way to handle the concern would be to get the cooperation of all the neighbors on the street and approach the company again. We needed better reasons and facts to support our position. We needed better arguments to win the company over to our point of view. So we drafted a letter and had every person in the neighborhood sign it. They included their name and address. The letter explained the problem, what the change meant to them, and how it introduced new challenges for some of the elderly residents.

Then we asked for a simple form of relief. We asked that the manager reschedule our entire street to either Tuesday or Wednesday morning. The response was quick and precise.

They agreed.

Within a week the schedule was changed. The problem was resolved. By organizing the neighbors we got what we wanted. When Mary acted alone, she got nowhere.

However, together as a united coalition we developed a clear message that explained the problem. In our letter we documented the situation and demonstrated an understanding of the facts from their point of view. We also acknowledged that we understood the company's position. We explained how the new policy combined with the ordinance was harming their customers. We had determined that the City Council members would not repeal the law and enforcement and fines would be forthcoming and probably escalate if there were complaints and continuing infractions.

Seems simple so far, right?

All of this was done in a professional and polite manner. We didn't just set out the problem; we provided alternative solutions for the company, and we explained why the matter was important to us as customers of their service.

From the company's point of view, it was a no-brainer. They had a small but focused neighborhood force, – more than a dozen customers paying them thousands of dollars a year—they could authenticate us by name and address so they knew we were real customers. The group had articulated a new problem that was the result of the company's recent policy change. And as a group, we provided a solution and made it easy for the company to act. Also, they knew we weren't going away.

So all three elements worked together. (1) We had a clear message. (2) We had agreement among the neighbors. (3) And we had the resources to get our issue in front of the right person (the decision-maker) at the right time. Plus, we were paying customers.

But you might ask, what if this hadn't worked? Did we have other remedies? Yes, including everything from talking to our local City Council, to peer pressure, to gathering a larger number of people (including professional senior citizen advocacy organizations) and bringing in other neighborhood groups.

Fortunately we didn't have to resort to Plan B. Why? Because we had a worthwhile and compelling case. We made everything simple, clear, and precise. It was easy for the company to decide to make the change. There was no downside or real operational cost to them.

The message here is simple. If you act alone, you get nothing done.

It can be frustrating and difficult to make change. But if you get the cooperation of like-minded people who have a common goal, it's easier to clarify an issue and coalesce around it. When that is done, one or two people can then take the lead and take direct action with a company, a politician or whomever you want to influence. It also helps to have a Plan B.

I cite this as a simple example of grassroots advocacy because all the required pieces of influence were applied during this small but successful community action.

Case #2 –
Susan's Car Wash Exemption – A County Issue

A business acquaintance of mine, I'll call her Susan, owns a small retail chain of gas stations and minimarts. She employs more than 100 people. She wanted to add a carwash to one of her locations. There was not a carwash within 20 miles. In her other locations Susan's company used recycled water and met all the EPA and state environmental standards but because of several environmental rules and other zoning issues, she needed the approval of the county.

Local residents wanted a closer, more convenient carwash. Susan was a good corporate citizen and supported California's 80% drought reduction rules advocated by Carwash.org/water savers.

Susan knew what she had to do.

She met personally with every member of the five-person County supervisors. They had authority to grant her a license to improve the location. As is often the case, she had two yeas, two nays and one hold out.

There was nothing she could offer Supervisor Ben, the holdout, to convince him that there would be a community benefit that would help him and the rest of the town. But the supervisor made it clear that he was up for reelection and he wouldn't mind if Susan made a campaign contribution.

This is where the story gets a little fuzzy. You have to keep policy "asks" separate from political campaign contributions.

Susan did. But that wasn't enough. Next, the politician, Ben wanted other favors that Susan wasn't willing to agree to. It's OK to ask a politician for their vote on a specific issue. It's not OK to couple that with a contingent relationship between the vote and a financial contribution. In fact quid pro quo ("this for that") is illegal. Susan and the supervisor both knew this. Under normal circumstances, ethical politicians don't tolerate *quid pro quo* ("you scratch my back and I'll scratch yours).

We spoke. I told her how I would approach this problem. It was clear to me that she had some, but not all of the following must-haves.

1. Message – She had a clearly articulated message about what she wanted to achieve.
2. Mass – Although she had a small executive team, and a few others who supported the cause, she did not have a lot of voters in her corner.
3. Money – She had the financial resources to withstand a drawn-out battle and was willing to engage if push came to shove.

So her weakest area was #2, having a sufficient number of constituents in the district that would support her. But that was easy enough to solve. She knew she had thousands of customers with dirty cars, trucks and vans who came through her store and gas stations on a weekly basis and she had dozens of employees who lived in the county.

In a series of meetings with the reluctant supervisor she hinted that if he would like to see broader community support she could arrange for hundreds of her customers and his voters to show up in their unwashed pickup trucks at the open public county meeting to express their support for the new car wash.

They would explain how this would help solve the water issue, make it more convenient for them and increase the tax revenue for the county.

The last thing the supervisor wanted was public participation by hundreds of voters and tradesman on a small, non-contentious issue right before his election. It could be embarrassing because his numbers were low and it would show he did not support the community. It might even call press attention to his anti small business and anti-jobs position in a county also struggling with employment issues.

As it turned out, she didn't need to round up her customers to get them to sign a petition or agree to help her out or drive their dusty vehicles to the county seat.

In the end, it wasn't a long battle. It was a conversation. No favors were passed. No litigation was involved. And the community benefited by having another facility and car wash closer in their area that made it more convenient for everyone and added a few more jobs. The county also increased their tax revenue, and the supervisor was reelected.

A few months later supervisor Ben's campaign staff approached Susan about helping him pay down his reelection campaign expenses. I don't know if she contributed or not. But she still has a carwash and he is still in office.

Case #3 –
Kate's Tarmac Rule - Flyers Rights –
Federal Consumer Issue

Like many passengers tired of being treated poorly by airlines, Kate Hani decided to found the consumer advocacy group, Flyer's Rights. The group came together over common problems such as flyers waiting endlessly on a tarmac, lost luggage fees, airline reimbursement, hidden fees etc. Instead of just complaining, they outlined specific recommendations they wanted to see addressed and referred to this as the Passenger Bill of Rights or the so-called "Tarmac Rule".

There was enough public outcry that the coalition gained the attention of the Department of Transportation, (the agency that regulates the airlines).

On April 29, 2010, the Department of Transportation (DOT) adopted new regulations for the airlines. This was a series of pro-passenger DOT airline regulations. The EU (European Union) also adopted similar standards. This is a case where legislative change did not occur but rather was implemented through a DOT ruling. This was a project brought about through public pressure and media attention.

A clear and specific message and a large base of organized support helped contribute to this success. This is a case of defensive lobbying and coalition building in an effort to protect consumers. Clear message, grassroots advocacy and the resources and energy to see it through.

Case #4 –
Bill's Porsche - Special Vehicle Exemption –
Federal Agency Regulation

I recently saw a segment on CNBC, which discussed some of the things that wealthy people spend their money on.

It showcased Microsoft founder Bill Gates who wanted to buy a rare Porsche 959. The car was not street legal and could not be imported into the United States. But Mr. Gates really wanted the car.

A "Special Vehicles Coalition" was formed to frame their arguments and position, discuss the issue and educate the rule makers.

The coalition then hired the Washington DC lobbying firm Dyer Ellis. According to the Center for Responsive Politics, which reports on lobbying expenditures, in 1998 Dyer Ellis reported receiving about $20,000 from the Special Vehicles Coalition.

The firm navigated their way through government bureaucracy. That's what lobbyists do. The firm's efforts resulted in what eventually became known as the Show or Display Rule, which exempts specific vehicles and allows them to be imported into the US. This became a statutory amendment under the Federal Motor Vehicle Safety Standards Act. Bill could get his car.

Imported vehicles eligible under the rules were reviewed and managed by the National Highway Traffic Safety Administration (NHTS). Imported cars also needed to meet certain Environmental Protection Agency, EPA standards. The rule became law on August 13, 1999 under 49 U.S. Code § 30114 public law 103–272 section 1e.

In the end by changing the rules, Gates was able to legally import the car. Any other vehicles that met the same standard would also qualify to be imported. So the rule applied not only to him, but also to other rare car buyers.

I include this because I want you to understand what constitutes success and also to show you that this is completely achievable.

Why did this work? There was a clear and specific message, backed up with logical arguments and real voters. The coalition came together in significant enough numbers and contributed funds to support the advocacy effort. The cost to accomplish this was not that high. They hired an expert firm to represent them. Even though these were smart, capable people they still brought in experts in government relations. There was little opposition to the rule change. So the government was able to accommodate the coalition's request. And that's how things get done.

Case #5 –
Lew's Video Piracy – Federal Issue

As I mentioned previously, in the early 1990s I worked in government affairs at MCA. MCA was the corporate parent for Universal Studios and all of the Universal properties; film, television, music, videos, theme parks etc. When I was there technology was transitioning from the analog VCR to digital media. Because it made copying easy, the studios were concerned about the piracy of digital media. Countries that didn't subscribe to international copyright laws and standards (The Berne Convention) had no problem ignoring the rules.

Pirates could simply duplicate any song, film, book, etc. at almost no cost. In the music industry, this came to a head with the peer-to-peer networks and the rise of Napster and other file-sharing sites in the early 2000's.

There were stories about digital Pirates who would go into theaters and record full-length movies with portable video cameras. They would then ship the digital copies overseas to non-signatory countries. Even some signed countries did not enforce the law. They had more important problems than copyright enforcement on behalf of American intellectual property owners. These bootleg recordings of movies and music became very common and cost the industry hundreds of millions of dollars.

The financial losses affected everyone in the industry; actors, directors, stagehands, lighting, union grips, transportation folks etc. Since no licensing fees were paid, the industry started to feel the pain.

At first the studios tried to solve the problem from a technical standpoint but eventually turned to the government for help.

It was a complex, multifaceted problem but in the end, key trade bills were written, sponsored and passed in the House of Representatives and U.S. Senate. They effectively provided trade sanctions against violators. These policy changes came into place because of three crucial elements:

1. Message – The entertainment industry could no longer tolerate the theft of its intellectual property (movies, music etc.) because piracy had an economically adverse effect on the film industry, one of the largest exporters of American culture abroad, and an industry with a positive balance of trade.
2. Mass – Studio heads came together with the support of the affected unions, actors, government, etc. Everybody supported the bills that protected the creation and legal distribution of their work.
3. Money – The studios had the financial wherewithal, the intellectual acumen, and the political and legal pressure (pretty much 100% of Hollywood) to move the legislation forward by working closely with the government and the legislators. The studios also had the support of trade associations like the Motion Picture Association, with Jack Valenti and other lobbying firms. They helped to articulate the message and present their case to the politicians and administration and successfully navigate the halls of Congress.

Ultimately, billions of dollars were saved when the legislation went into effect and became law.

In the end you need to work with, not against, the government if you want to get anything done.

Policy Success

You may have uncertainty about your personal cause. But everyone does at first. No one has everything figured out before they start. But once you start you become a cause set in motion. And you see it through to completion. You finish the job. Why? Because policy matters. You are motivated to make it happen. This is change that *you* want. So you start.

"Policy Success = motivation + initiative + commitment."

If you compare yourself to someone else and find that they are better, smarter, and richer, then you will be determined to find a way to take positive action toward your goal of becoming better, smarter and more prosperous.

Self-initiative is a driving force that comes from comparing and contrasting yourself to others. We do this all the time. If you are dissatisfied with the status quo and how things are, then you'll turn your attention into action. Self-initiative plus self-reflection moves you forward.

You need to be dissatisfied enough with how things are. Otherwise you will never start. And if you are committed enough to a cause, you will keep going. Nothing can stand in your way.

These five cases show how you can pull together the elements to move legislation forward using constituent advocacy.

All three elements are prerequisites for success to happen and are thus always present in winning advocacy efforts.

You can think of this process like a recipe. You need the correct ingredients (in our case message, mass and money) and you need a sequential procedure that combines the ingredients in a way that produces the best results.

So can you do this? Yes.

Can anyone do it? Yes. You don't have to know everything before you start.

But above all, you need to start.

Final Thoughts – There Oughta' Be a Law

In 2000 when California State Senator Joe Simitian was elected to office in (CA-AD-21) (California Assembly District 21) he wanted to find a way to get input from his almost 1,000,000 constituents in Silicon Valley.

He came upon the idea of using an incentive contest to encourage voters to submit their ideas for new laws or laws that should be taken off the books. He called the contest "There Oughta' Be a Law ." (http://www.senatorsimitian.com/oughta/)

He successfully ran this from 2001 to 2012 while he was in office and during that time he ended up with several hundred submissions. Of these he would select the ones that had the highest likelihood of community interest and support. In all, 18 citizen proposals became law.

On the site it states, *"Contest winners are invited to the State Capitol for lunch with State Senator Simitian and will have an opportunity to testify on behalf of their bill at a formal hearing. Each winner will also receive a California State flag that has been flown over the Capitol. But the real prize is knowing that your idea has the potential of becoming law for 38 million Californians."*

Several key bills came out of citizen legislator initiatives, one of which was SB 1538 Comprehensive Breast Cancer Screening for women in 2013, SB 1303 Red Light Camera Reform, SB 802 Masking All But the Last Five Digits of a Debit Card Number on a Business Receipt, and many others.

The contest was a success. It encouraged citizen engagement and gave voters a new way to connect with their lawmakers.

When he left office in 2012 you would think that would have been the end of the contest. However, several other lawmakers heard of it and picked up on the idea. Today, California Senator Jerry Hill, (CA-SD-13), Assemblywoman Catherine Baker, (CA-AD-16) and others from both parties have continued the effort in their districts.

But it did not end there.

A few state lawmakers in Pennsylvania got wind of this. They used a similar format and made it available to their citizens. They include Senators Sean Wiley (PA-SD-49), Ryan Aument (PA-SD-36) and Pennsylvania State House of Representatives' legislator Thomas Murt (PA-R-152), Tim Briggs (PA-D-149), and Marcia Hahn (PA-R-138).

Even a Central Manor elementary school teacher in Pennsylvania decided the contest was a good idea. In 2012 she made it available to her fourth grade class.

She encouraged her students, future young voters, to take a less formal approach and write a simple essay about what they thought would be a good law for Pennsylvania.

In 2013 Paige Flinchbaugh presented her law essay about exercise for students as it related to the growing problem of child obesity. It won the contest in the class. It was submitted to then House Member Ryan Aument who read it, reviewed it, liked it and thought it would be a good idea for the community.

He took the essay to the next level. He sponsored it in the Pennsylvania state legislature. The essay was re-drafted and turned into a Legislative Reference Bureau format and was then introduced on the floor in the Pennsylvania Senate in 2013. In its final form it amended a public law, the Act P.L. 30 (No. 14). The thrust of the bill was that it helped students increase their exercise time at school so that they could be more active and healthy.

Paige Flinchbaugh was praised for her initiative, decision-making and clarity of thought. Recall, she was in the fourth grade and she was only 10 years old.

Representative Ryan Aument interviewed her and posted the interview on YouTube (https://www.youtube.com/watch?v=MPdzwfZTGOU). Her law is in effect today.

The message I want to leave with you is really quite simple. If you are frustrated by the political system, take action. Instead of assuming that you are unable to make a difference and your voice does not matter, take a new approach.

Remember, if a 10-year-old can do it, you can too.

Chapter 6

LET'S DEMYSTIFY POLITICS

~ STEP 6 ~

Time required: 30 minutes

~ DAY 6 ~

Complete your profile so it really reflects you.
Read the quick-start Debate Writer's Guide PDF.
Then start your own debate.

"I know of no country in which there is so little independence of mind and real freedom of discussion as in America."
~Alexis de Tocqueville (1805-1859)~

"Life's most persistent and urgent question is, 'What are you doing for others?'"
~Martin Luther King, Jr.~

There are several myths about lobbying and politics that I would like to share with you. I have heard these over and over again from different people but for the most part they are not true. Some reflect internal doubts we have. Others are incorrect perceptions about the process and the profession.

So let's start busting some of these myths.

Myths about message

Myth #1 - *"One of the biggest myths we have is that lobbyists are bad."* - This could also include public affairs and government relations' consultants. If they are so bad, then why do corporations, unions, trade associations, nonprofits, state governments and special interests continue to hire them to get their message out to the lawmakers?

You might note that you don't see lobbyists or government affairs professionals shouting slogans, marching on the Washington Mall, holding up protest signs, signing petitions, calling talk radio or disrupting town halls. Ever wonder why?

Myth #2 - *"I don't have any issues."* - This is a critical one because it goes along with the thinking of "Since I don't have any issues, I don't care and I do not need to be involved." Chances are you do have issues; you're just not aware of them. I assure you there is no aspect of your life that is untouched by the government at some level. Just look around your community. You will find it easy to see things that need to be improved. In fact according to the Competitive Enterprise Institute, the annual regulatory burden on business is $1.2 trillion and costs each household $15,000 per year.

Myth #3 - *"The political problems are beyond fixing. So there's nothing I can do."* - This is a self-perpetuating and disempowering falsehood. You have been misinformed and disengaged for so long that you now believe there's nothing you can do. Yet nothing could be farther from the truth. You just need to figure out your message. This is the same kind of thinking as saying "I have nothing to say, nothing to contribute. My voice does not matter." It's just not true.

__Myth #4__ - "The politician says he will deliver what he promises while campaigning." – Voters often want to believe the political campaign promises of the candidate they vote for. And thus the voters look no further. Rarely do they look at issues and accomplishments of the candidate. Yet, they are naïvely eager to believe the campaign promise.

__Myth #5__ - "The politician says she supported that issue and she voted for the bill but she could not get it through because the other Party was against it." – Voters constantly fall for this story. So they don't hold their leaders accountable. By shifting blame from the elected official to the other party, the politician is able to deflect criticism and show that she too is powerless in a very complex political system. But if you just give her another chance, more money, more time and reelect her (because there is a lot of work yet to be done), then she will try harder next time. Sound familiar?

__Myth #6__ - "Protesters, demonstrators and people who sign petitions know what they want." - Sometimes this is true, often it is not. Many protesters are paid to be there. They don't believe in the message. They just show up, shout slogans and hold signs. They are paid by someone else to do it. When people gather petitions, not always but many times, they too don't believe in the message. They are paid by an organization and they are paid per signature. They are just selling someone else's idea. So don't be fooled by the apparent strength in numbers.

Myths about mass

__Myth #7__ - "Our leaders know what is best for us." – This statement includes a few subareas. Politics is complicated. Let's leave it to the experts. Let's leave it to the pros. Our leaders will be fair. We, the American people are too uninformed to understand policy enough to govern ourselves. We really don't want a bunch of ignorant people running the country. We don't want mob rule or mobocracy.

This represents a whole collection of disempowering beliefs.

It assumes that there is a noble benefactor somewhere out there looking out for your best interest. Chances are this mythic white knight does not exist. But you keep looking, and ignore the fact that special interest groups will continue to control the agenda so long as you do not engage. They are counting on your passivity. Don't fall into this trap.

Myth #8 - *"The president has the power to solve every problem through executive action."* – This is the same as the issue above. It just personifies the solution into one person, the president. This thinking prevents us from seeking active resolution through our representative. This is the myth of the omnipotent director, Superman, who can save us from everything. This belief is completely false yet it remains a major myth that many people buy into.

Myth #9 - *"You have to be an attorney to do this."* – No, actually you don't. You can enlist legal help as you go along but you do not have to be a lawyer to have an idea. The founder of Mothers Against Drunk Driving (MADD), Candy Lightner was not an attorney yet she was instrumental in implementing the National Minimum Drinking Age Act (NMDAA). The family advocate for Amber Alerts was not an attorney, yet they were able to pass the Amber Hagerman Child Protection Act. In fact there are many public affairs consultants who believe in a cause but are not lawyers. Just like you don't have to be a doctor to understand your health, you don't have to be a mechanic to fix your car and you don't have to get a real estate license to sell your home. You bring in the experts as you need them but it is not required for you to become a licensed expert in order to start and be successful.

Myth #10 - *"It's all about who you know. Powerful people control policy."* – While this is generally true, it doesn't always work out to the benefit of a specific individual or group. Remember, voters elect members of Congress. If enough voters are knowledgeable and dissatisfied with the votes of their representative, they can vote the politician out of office. So, congressional members want to have input from their constituents, not just the special interests.

Myth #11 - "I really don't care about politics. I'm not committed and I can't do it." - Well, you certainly can't do it alone. And that's one of our central ideas. Perhaps you became frustrated after your repeated advocacy efforts proved ineffective. But one of the keys is, you have to work with other people to make things happen. You can't do it alone. You need to build a coalition of like-minded individuals.

Myths about money

Myth #12 - "Money in politics corrupts the process. We should get money out of politics." – On the surface, this seems to make sense. But most of the reporting around money focuses on campaign contributions, the electoral side, not the policy side. Candidates need money to run their campaigns and spread their message in tight races. Most of the money subsequently goes to organizing, staff and media buys. There is a general assumption that the largest donors will control the thoughts and votes of the elected politician.

However, this is not true.

This "quid pro quo" thinking may exist but it is false. If the will of the people is adverse to the will of the top donor, then the will of the people will prevail. But voters also need to contribute to candidates they support. They need to maintain a relationship with the politician and continue to educate and influence their representative while he is in office. It's not all about money.

So what I'm saying is not that we should take money out of politics but instead, we should have less concentration of money and a broader base of contributors who advocate on issues.

Myth #13 - "Lobbyists pay money to politicians and gain access." – For the most part this is false but the press keeps these kinds of stories alive because they are more interesting than the ordinary dull job of reporting on government affairs professionals. The lobbying industry is highly regulated and lobbyists publicly report all their activity. Many don't have PACs (political action committees) and do not make campaign contributions.

Myth #14 - *"Lobbyists can influence policy."* – Sometimes they can, but often they cannot. They win about the same number of bills as anyone else, only around 30%. They educate their clients and the politicians around issues, but they cannot force issues to resolve in their favor. Their job is to persuade.

Myth #15 - *"Get money out of politics. Instead, we need publicly funded elections."* - People are concerned about corruption and money in politics. But it's because of the concentration of the money. You may think that if money is removed from the process, somehow everything will be fine. Or if elections are publicly funded, everything will be fine. However, I do not think these are the solutions to the problem. In fact you don't need to remove money, you need to remove the concentration of capital.

You do this by broadening the base, or the number of people who contribute. Instead of spending money on campaigns, these funds could be used to hire a lobbyist to focus on moving a specific issue forward.

Myth #16 - *"You're making this all too simple."* – If what I am talking about seems oversimplified, I am OK with that. You may think that I am giving people false hope by making all of this appear simpler than it really is. Well you're right. I am. If I tell you how hard and complex the process really is, you might not even try and that's where we are now.

But, if we are determined enough, we can find ways to make the hard things work. Building skyscrapers is hard, performing open-heart surgery is hard, propelling rockets into space is hard, and conducting an international corporate merger is hard. Just because something is hard doesn't mean we don't try. Trying enables us to find people who are skilled and available to take on these very large and complex tasks.

Changing a law in your local community may be simpler than changing a law at the federal level. But both are possible. It happens every day.

The sooner the American people are exposed to these myths and move past them, the better off we will be. You need to accept that your political destiny lies in your own hands.

Chapter 7

A RADICAL
NEW SOLUTION

~ STEP 7 ~

Time required: 1 minute

~ DAY 7 ~

Publish your debate and congratulate yourself!
Your voice counts.

> *"Our lives begin to end the day we become
> silent about things that matter."*
>
> **~Martin Luther King, Jr.~**

Getting started – The iLobby Platform

So this is what you have been waiting for. Let's start right now. Remember, we are using the iLobby platform as the basis for taking you through this seven-step program. To keep it simple, I am going to assume that you are using a desktop or a laptop and not a mobile device.

As I have previously mentioned, there are three elements needed to succeed. They are (1) message, (2) mass and (3) money.

In this chapter I will take you through step-by-step how to make sure you have all three in alignment.

I will weave these three elements into the seven steps so that by the end of this chapter you'll have a clear message about an issue you want to pursue. You will also know how to begin attracting followers and sponsors to your cause and you can begin pulling the necessary resources together to advance your campaign.

Let's begin.

Step number one – sign up and vote on one debate

Go to https://www.ilobby.co (It's .co, *not* .com.)

I am assuming at this point that you are logged in. If you are not, then you will need to login at the very top where you see the small login link. You can sign up directly or you can sign up through Facebook.

Find a debate on the website. In this case we will use the debate on drones as we walk through the seven steps.

Anonymous users

Anonymous users can't vote. Just like in real life you have to be a US citizen over 18 and you have to register if you want to vote. So, if you want to vote, comment, argue, or start a debate you need to register on the site.

The debate card

Scroll down and you should find the drone debate that says "*Support H.R. 3669 – Safe Drone Act of 2015.*"

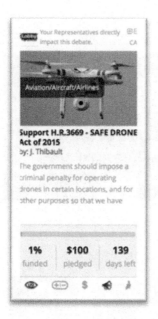 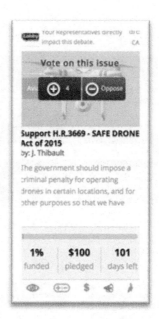

If you are on the desktop and hover over the card, two buttons will appear, a red and a green button. These are your voting buttons. If you are on a mobile device or a tablet the green and red voting buttons will already be visible.

You should notice a couple of things about the card. An image of the person or organization that started this debate will be visible in the upper left-hand corner. The state that they're from will be to the far right.

Over the photograph you will see a category, in this case it says *Aviation/ Aircraft/Airlines*. This is the actual issue code that the Senate uses for categorizing lobbying activity. There are 78 of these codes in total.

Below the picture is the title. "*Support H.R. 3669 - Safe Drone Act of 2015.*" The word "*support*" tells us the author's position. H.R. means it is a house resolution and the actual bill number is 3669. The short title of the proposed act is Safe Drone Act of 2015.

Then right below that is the name of the debate creator or author. There is a very brief top-level summary and text right below. The number of days left for the debate and the amount of money pledged to this specific cause are shown at the bottom.

If you are already logged in and have created any activity in this debate, your activity will show up in blue in the five icons at the very bottom of the card. Otherwise, the icons will be gray.

From left to right these are:
- Eye - you are following this debate (You are keeping an eye on it)
- A voting indicator (+/-) button - you have voted on it
- $ - You have pledged money
- Megaphone - you have added an argument
- Thumbs up - you liked this debate

So let's click on the text title "Support H.R. 3669" and go into the debate.

The debate overview

In the upper left-hand corner of this page, (below the header menu) you will see the title again. Right below it will say: "Summary" "Arguments" and "Committee."

Note: this debate appears in the tab My Debates because I was the author. Otherwise it would appear under All Debates.

To the right of the photograph there is a short impact statement. Above the word "Impact" you will see some sharing icons that we will talk about in step five.

On the right side you will see the author information. We include the author's name, avatar, a link to their bio or profile as well as the Congressional District they live in. In this case it's California 18, which is Representative Anna Eshoo's district. More about this later.

Below this we see the level of funding, the votes and pledging. We will talk about this in step four.

Right below the photograph you will see the debate summary and additional information.

Familiarize yourself with this and see if you can form an opinion on this proposed piece of legislation.

Right below, there are two columns. One column says "Sources That Support", while the other column says "Sources That Oppose." Below each column are websites and videos which link to appropriate sources.

Under "Sources That Support", look at Websites. Click the first website link "Safe Drones Act 2015."

This will take you to the government website congress.gov. Here you can explore many aspects about the bill. For those who want the current status and the actual wording it is available here.

Read the headline about the issue. Then click on the text title and it will take you to the full document. Here you can read the impact, summary etc. so that you have an understanding of what the issue is about.

This US government page shows legislation in the House and the Senate. I won't go into the details on this page but in the tabs there are a couple things to notice.

You will see the sponsor of the bill and the date that the bill was introduced. You will also notice the committees that the bill falls under and the latest actions/status of the bill.

Below this are eight tabs: Summary, Text, Actions, Titles, Amendments, Cosponsors, Committees, and Related Bills.

These will become important as we move further along.

At this point the bill is written in the legislative bureau form language or what you and I would refer to as legalese. You don't need to read this but I want you to be aware that it is here.

Let's go back to the iLobby site.

In the sources that support and sources that oppose, go ahead and click through as many of the website and video links as you want. When a person writes a debate, they are including this information to inform you, not to propagandize you.

That's why both sides of the issue are shown. We want you to make up your own mind about what you think the right answer is.

The reason that the author has included so many links is to reduce the overall research you will need to do in order to educate yourself on this issue. The author has already done this research by presenting you with sources that both support and oppose his view.

Once you feel like you have an opinion and know what your position is, then you are ready to vote.

We have included the vote buttons in the upper right-hand corner of the page and they function the same way as they did on the smaller card on the first homepage you saw.

Once you are logged in, vote on the issue by clicking either the red or green button to indicate your support or opposition for the bill.

 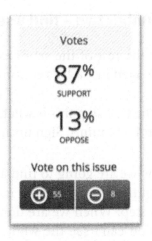

The vote count and the percentage will change automatically.
Also keep in mind that you can only vote once per debate.
That's it.
So let's reflect on this for a moment.

Summary

You have identified an issue you care about. You became informed about the issue. You have looked at both sides of the issue from independent and government sources. You have looked at the actual bill and the bill language. You have a beginner understanding of the meaning of the congressional language surrounding a bill.

You have identified your position on this specific issue. And your position is really one of two, either you support the bill language or you do not support it. But by taking action by voting on this issue, you are affirming your position for this specific bill.

If you reflect on this, you are 10 steps ahead of everybody else because you have a deeper understanding of the issue, you have been thoughtful in looking at it and you are beginning to align yourself with one side or the other.

Congratulations.

Step number two – find a second debate and vote

For the rest of the set of exercises I am going to assume that you are logged in. So let's continue.

In the first step this is what you had to do:
Step 1 - (4 min.) Sign up at iLobby and vote on one debate.

Now we are going to find a second debate and vote on it. The important thing to remember is that each of the steps builds on the previous step. When we are done, we pull it all together. It's like a puzzle. You can't see the whole picture until you start putting all the pieces together in the right order.

Step 2 - (3 min.) Find a second debate and vote on it.
Are you with me? So, here we go.
From the homepage https://www.ilobby.co find a debate that has a number of days left on it. If there are zero days left, then you cannot vote.

Remember, if you want to vote on a debate, then you want one that is still open. Once you find a debate, hover over the photograph or the debate card. The red and green voting box will appear and you can click on one side or the other to either support the general idea or oppose it. Essentially, you are making a decision about how you would cast your vote if you were faced with this issue.

Another way of looking at this is that you are informing your Representative about this issue and your position on it.

If you hover over the debate card and the voting box comes up as blue or gray, this indicates that you have already voted on this issue. But just like a politician, you can still change your mind. You can change your vote up until the final vote is counted when the debate ends.

Now, this may all seem foreign to you because you are used to voting for candidates instead of issues.

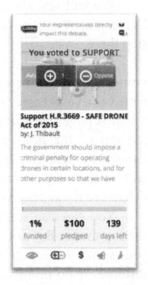

But if you think about it, that's exactly what elected politicians do every day. They gather the facts about an issue from multiple sources and constituents, and they sift through all the information and data. Then they make their decision and cast their vote.

What we are doing here is having you replicate those behaviors. But this is not direct democracy. Your vote is not counted in Congress or the legislature. You have elected a representative for that. But by voting here, your vote will be aggregated with other constituents in your district and can be used to inform your representative about your collective position. We will go into the power of building an ad hoc coalition and running a campaign later on. But for the time being, let's stay with the task at hand.

Previously, I talked about how important this is. If you can begin to think of yourself as a *"citizen legislator,"* or even just an average person who is informed and has opinions about issues, then you can begin to shape the issues and cause the dialogue to move one way or the other. Your vote is not insignificant.

Think about it. If millions of people voted on a regular basis on specific issues, then in aggregate their information would inform the lawmakers about how they think about an issue. You wouldn't have to write to your member of Congress to let him or her know because you will have already indicated your support or opposition by voting.

This saves you time because you can do it quickly. This saves them effort because they don't have to open your letter, read it, validate who you are and then have their staff respond. This takes you out of the isolation of solitary action and puts you into a social/political coalition that has one voice.

We will talk about how you can actually shape the proposed legislation by adding an argument of your own in the next step, step three.

But for now, look at the debates or the debate cards on the homepage and make a quick assessment of what you think aligns with your values and vote on it. If there's nothing that you see on this first page that you have an opinion about then go to the tab at the top of the homepage and click on Discover Great Debates (https://www.ilobby.co/debates/grid). Here you will find more choices. In fact, at the very bottom of the page you can go through all the debates that have been created.

You can also search by keyword, category or ZIP Code from the top menu. But at this point, and in most cases this will narrow your search too much and you probably will not find anything. For instance, if no one from your specific ZIP Code created a debate then if you enter your ZIP Code, you will come up blank.

As more debates are created this will become less of an issue.

If you use the category search to find more debates, here's an example of how it might work. Click on the category drop-down box. Scroll down to "Homeland Security." Then click on the search icon to the right. A few debates in this category will come up.

While we are looking at this category drop down box, I want to mention the following. You might be asking yourself where these category names come from. Well these are the actual 78 issue codes that the U.S. Senate uses when lobbying firms report on the issues that they are advocating for. By mapping our categories to what the government is using, it will become easier for you to match your issue with what other advocates are promoting.

As a side note, there are differences between the federal and state lobbying issue codes. In some cases there is overlap. And others are completely different. This is just the beginning of where things begin to get complex. And our mantra is to keep things simple.

So your task for today is to find an open debate, and simply vote on it by clicking either support or oppose, using the red or green button.

I want you to see how easy this is, how quickly you can do it, and how accessible this can be.

Remember, this really isn't about wasting your time. After all it only took a minute or less. But if thousands and thousands of people use up that extra minute of time and vote on a single debate the impact can be huge. And remember you can only vote once per debate. One person, one vote.

So if you've done that then we are ready to go on to step three.

Step three - Add an argument

Now we are going to add an argument. So what is an argument? Well, it's actually a statement or a comment that you make that either supports the main thesis or opposes it.

When you voted in step one and step two, you indicated that you either agree or disagree with the main idea or the main thrust of what the debate author has stated.

You were only indicating your position. You were saying "Yes I agree" or "No I completely disagree." But you were not giving any specific reason as to why. Which is fine.

But now you might want to delve in a little more deeply because the debate card only provides a very short summary of the information. To find out more click on the debate card title and go in to the full debate. You know you are there because it will say "Debate Summary." You will see a short impact statement, the debate summary, additional information perhaps and sources including websites and videos that support and/or oppose.

The idea here is to have everything in one place, so that if you are interested in a topic or a controversial issue, you don't have to go searching all over the Internet to do the primary research. The debate author has already done that for you, hopefully.

Perhaps you share a personal story that applies to this issue.

Your position

So when you are ready to add your comment or to make an argument, you have a choice. By now you should have a clear idea of whether you support or oppose this particular issue and the way the author has framed it. This will determine where you post your argument and what side of the column you are on.

After you have read the extra information in the debate summary and have looked at the links of the information that the author proposed; now it's time for you to click on the second tab at the top called "Arguments."

At the top you will see arguments in support versus arguments in opposition. This is where you get to speak up, take a stand, and tell the world what you think and why your point of view matters. This does not have to be a deep analysis of the issue. In fact, we actually discourage that.

Some of you might be disappointed that we have limited the number of characters to a short burst of information similar to what you could post on Twitter. But we have given you an out.

If you discover that 120 characters is not enough space to share your opinion on this topic then here's what you can do. You can use a link shortener like bit.ly or owl.ly.

We have found that readers prefer to read short, pithy comments. But I also recognize the value of having a more substantial argument that supports what it is that you want to say. So we have tried to accommodate both worlds.

Your first choice is to decide, do you want to create an argument on the support side or do you want to create an argument on the opposition side?

If you are creating an argument that supports the author's intent then you are affirming and helping him win over more people to that side of the debate. But if you think the author has left out important information, has incorrect facts or you completely oppose what he is saying, then you should create your argument on the opposition side.

The readers who come in after you will be able to see both sides of the issue if many people contributed comments. This gives the voters the ability to decide for themselves what they think the right answer is. And isn't that the point of a debate? How many of us love having someone ram his or her ideas down our throats? We don't.

I think we want the ability to look at all sides of an issue and then come to our own conclusion. And that's the point of having a global, open online debate.

Link shortener

Let me quickly explain how to use the link shortener websites. If you have a great piece or an article on your blog that you would like to link/share but the link is longer than the limited 120 characters you are provided, then you need to use a link shortener. First of all, copy the link or URL from your long research paper, blog or other source that you want to include. Then go to bitly.com and paste your link into their system. They will automatically convert your link into a much shorter one. You can now take this very short link and add it in the argument field where you are making your comment.

And that's it.

After you have made your comment or argument, click the small megaphone and your argument will be posted.

Once posted, you can "like" your argument with the thumbs up symbol. You can also "like" other people's arguments if you agree with them. Or you may tweet your own argument to attract more interest. We will talk a little bit more about sharing in step five.

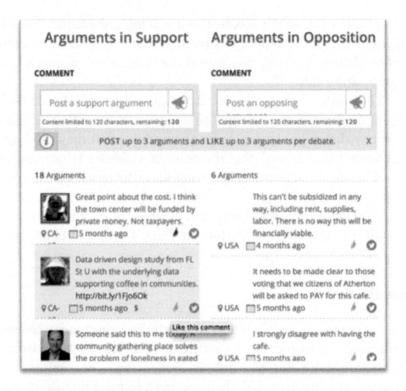

Now, let's say someone comments on your argument and they dispute what you have to say. Which happens all the time. Well guess what? You get to add another argument. In fact you can add a total of three arguments. So make your arguments count.

Three arguments

Why only three? We have found that there is some concern that certain groups might try to dominate a debate by spamming it with their users in a very one sided, deliberate and repetitive way. We believe that preventing one special interest group from dominating the conversation will help maintain fairness by giving every person the opportunity to contribute their opinion and have it be seen. After all, that is the point of democracy.

Ad hominem attacks

The other problem area that occurs is when individuals start attacking one another and the debate devolves into chaos. If everyone starts calling each other an idiot instead of providing insightful and educated comments, then the debate is not going to get very far.

We think this scenario occurs when the users are anonymous and can say whatever they want. That's not what we have here. We have authenticated users. If you truly want to make a difference in your political district then at some point you have to step up as a real person and be recognized for who you are. You have the autonomy to say what you want but we hope that intelligence prevails over diatribe.

We believe that combining authenticity with autonomy will produce efficacy in the issue deliberation process. We also think that if users do resort to invective, then eventually a user may be flagged for comment abuse.

After all, what are we trying to accomplish? We want to help solve global challenges that are affecting all of us. We want to provide informed dialog to our leaders so that they can make good decisions about public policy. We recognize that the laws that they make affect all of us, and we are paying for all these programs. So therefore we should have a greater say. When we come in as an uninformed mob, we are not helping anybody and we are certainly not helping ourselves.

So, to recap. You have voted on at least a couple of issues that you have an opinion about. You have created a very simple argument on one issue where you feel you can contribute something.

I think that you should be proud of yourself. If you have taken these first simple actions, then each step along the way shows a greater level of commitment. Hopefully, this has not been too hard. You have supported someone who took the time to create a debate and you have indicated your support.

A couple of other things to keep in mind.

Privacy

When you vote, your vote is private. Just like in real life. No one knows how you voted on an issue. When you make a comment or argument, then you are actually standing up, stating who you are, what district you are in and making your comment. No different then a Facebook post. No one has access to your email address. They just see what you have publicly stated, just like they would in a real Townhall.

So now let's go on to step four.

Step 4 - Pledge virtual currency

At this point you should be comfortable with the general layout of the Debate Card, the Debate Summary and the Arguments page.

Now let's move on to pledging.

On the right side of the Arguments page is an area where you can pledge virtual currency. Virtual currency? What is that?

Virtual currency

When we started, we assessed the idea of using real money and credit cards. However we pulled back from that for the time being. This is because the total amount of raised funds needed to hire a lobbyist on behalf of the coalition, is beyond the reach of the number of users currently on the site affecting any one debate. This is an issue of scale.

The point of using iLobby is to provide affordability and access to average voters so that they can get an inside pass to politicians by retaining public policy experts. But the services of public policy experts are generally very expensive and scarce. So they are costly, and therefore out of the reach of most voters.

But if we collectively pool our funds and we have a singular issue we are focused on, then we are in a much better position to discover, hire and retain a firm to represent your specific group.

There is a new breed of lobbyist who doesn't require a huge retainer and we think this is a good, voter friendly trend.

Play money

For the time being let's just consider virtual funding as "play money." Which it is. But it has a much more important purpose. It represents a proxy for your determination of the potential value that this law would mean to you. By removing real money from the equation we are doing two things:

1. We are removing the risk
2. And we are getting you used to the idea that there is value in your effort

In other words, if you want to get something done you have to put your money where your mouth is.

Every day we hear people complain that they don't have a say because special interests control the agenda and the rich are running the country and getting the laws that they want passed. Well if you're really serious about playing the game then you need to put some money into it to show your commitment.

But I don't want you to take my word for it just yet. I want you to get comfortable with the idea first. So what better way to play the game of politics then to do it with fictional funds.

You might think this is a complete waste of time. But, it is not. Every step along the way you are taking on a new but significant behavior. You are doing something that you have never done before. You are voting on an issue which in all likelihood many of us have never done before. You are making your position known. You are adding a comment into the public dialogue. And you're pledging a certain amount of virtual currency to a cause you believe in.

Think of it this way. If you could get a law passed that would have a great impact in your life or someone else's life, then how much would you be willing to contribute to make that happen? Five dollars, $10, $25, or more?

How much would you be willing to give up eventually? A couple of cups of coffee for a month, a movie ticket, attendance at a concert, a new pair of shoes? You probably never realized this, but there is a value associated with the laws that get passed and in the programs that get implemented. In fact the federal budget is about $3.8 trillion per year. As a taxpayer, we are paying for all of it.

For small business and individuals many of these costs associated with the regulations are passed on to us. We pay for them in filling out forms, time spent standing in lines, lost productivity, and government waste, fraud and abuse etc. Do you have any idea how much that costs? Well the regulatory burden is over $1 trillion per year according to the Competitive Enterprise Institute in their annual "10,000 Commandments" report. If this is correct then this is almost 30% of the annual federal budget. This breaks down to around $15,000 per year per household. So you're paying for it anyway even though you don't realize it.

Would you like to have a say in how that money is spent? Would you like to have a say in recovering some of the waste and putting more money in your pocket? Well there are people doing that all the time. You hear about them too. Large corporations that don't pay taxes, huge entities that keep cash overseas, the top 1% get a better tax rate than the average income earning individual. These groups are very involved in looking at laws, shaping public policy and deciding how things will run in the country. They are involved because they have an active interest in it and it is worth their time.

I would like to suggest that if it is worth their time, then it is also worth your time.

So all I'm asking you to do in step four is take one little step. And here it is.

Select a debate, any debate. Go into the debate summary.

Then in the column on the right that says virtual funding, select the tab and pick a certain amount of money. It could be five dollars, $10, $20, $50, or $100. At this point, it does not matter what you choose. Remember, this is not real money. No one is going to ask you to pay. This is a fictional amount with a purpose.

So select a dollar amount. Then hit the pledge button. A pledge confirmation box will appear confirming that you want to pledge or you may cancel. So go ahead and click "Send My Pledge Now."

Keep in mind you may only pledge once per debate.

Allowing users to pledge only small amounts and pledge only once prevents a large concerted special interest from controlling the pledging on a particular issue. So, one group cannot come in and pledge $1 million and then railroad everybody else's opinion.

But in order for this to work, many people need to step up and pledge small amounts to move an issue forward.

The future

What happens when we transition to real money?

In the future, pledges made will be collected and go into escrow. These funds will then be used by the creator of the debate to hire a lobbying firm to represent everyone who has contributed to this particular issue. But the minimum threshold must be met.

The money will not be used to support a politician. The money does not go to candidates for public office. The money is not distributed directly back to the person who started the debate.

Instead, the funds raised are held in a trust or in escrow and after a public policy firm or lobbying firm is hired by the person who started the debate, they authorize the payment of bills to the lobbyist on behalf of the group or coalition. If they think they need to raise more money to keep the issue moving forward, then they will have the opportunity to continue to raise more money through this crowd funding mechanism.

But we are not there yet. We'll talk more about this later.

So your task here in this step is really very simple. Select a debate. Pledge some virtual money. And now let's move on to step five.

Step five - Share a debate

You have now taken several concrete steps to understand an issue, get involved in it, and begin to step forward and clarify your thinking about what you really believe.

In this next step you are going to be a little more public by telling people that you support this particular issue. Are you ready? Here goes.

Once again, login to iLobby.

Then pick a debate, any debate and let's share it. I am going to pick the drone debate titled "Support H.R. 3669 – Safe Drone Act of 2015." From the main homepage or debate card click on the title. This will take you to the Debate Summary page. (https://www.ilobby.co/debate/support-hr3669-safe-drone-act-2015)

Right above the impact statement, in the center of the screen, you will see the sharing icons. From left to right they are as follows:

- Symbol of an eye – you're keeping an eye on this debate
- Paper airplane – share the debate via email
- G plus – share the debate on Google plus
- T – share the debate on Tumblr
- F – share the debate on Facebook
- Bird – share the debate on Twitter
- P – share the debate on Pinterest

If you want, you can share it to multiple sites. We have purposely made the titles relatively short so that you will have space to add a comment if you want.

In the case of this particular bill you could actually include the Chairman of the Committee's Twitter name. In this case it would be the Aviation Committee and the Chairman is Representative Frank LoBiondo from New Jersey or @RepLoBiondo. What would be the reason for including the name of the representative? You would bring your particular debate or any that you share to the respected members of the committee and their staff. Think about it. You can also share it with the press.

You never know where it will go from there. But sharing and sharing intelligently is a powerful way to get the word out about issues that you support or debates that you want to promote. You could also use the hashtag #iLobby.

If you are sharing someone else's debate, you are helping them out by giving them more exposure to your network.

In the next step we will talk about how to recognize the status of a sponsored bill and what committee it might be in.

Step 6 - Profile/Guide/Debate - Start a debate

Everything you have done up to this point has taken a very small amount of time. Well that is about to change.

If you like you can simply continue to do the first five steps. But if you really want to get your issue out there, and you really want to make a statement and you really want to change a law then you will need to proceed to this step and start your own debate.

So if you are up for a little hard work and you're committed, then this is for you.

Let's start by making sure that your profile is properly filled in.

Once you're logged in, from the homepage in the upper right-hand corner go to "My iLobby."

Fill in your profile

Your profile page will come up. Fill in the fields for your first name, last name and ZIP Code. When you're filling out your ZIP Code, it will automatically bring in your Congressional District. There are some districts that overlap ZIP Codes so you might find you do not have the right district and you can check it against the Find Your Congressional Representative site here (http://www.house. gov /representatives/find/).

You can also add a small 200 x 200 pixel picture or avatar of yourself, your company or your association logo.

Next in the About Me box fill in some information about yourself. This will be viewable to other members on the site. Next, we ask for your date of birth so that we know you are over the age of 18. Then, you can select your gender and political party. These fields and data are not used for advertising. They are there simply to help you find like-minded people in future versions of the service.

I previously talked about the 78 lobbying issue codes (https://lda.congress.gov/LD/help/default.htm?turl=Documents%2FAppCodes.htm) that the US Senate uses.

By selecting your top three issue areas, this will increase your chances of finding debates and issues that you are aligned with in the future.

Save your changes and that's it.

The Debate Writer's Guide

Next click on "Start a Debate" at the top of the page.

Right below the field where it says "Name your Debate", go ahead and click on the small blue link that says <u>Debate Writers Guide</u>. (https://www.ilobby.co/sites/default/files/ilobby-co-debate-writers-guide.pdf) This PDF will give you a quick overview of what steps you will need to go through as you begin to create your debate.

After you have read through it, you are ready to begin.

Finding your issue

Some of you already know what you want to write about. Others will get stuck right here. So I want to help you out and give you a framework for moving forward.

If you're looking at this and thinking you don't have any issues or no specific issue is important enough to you and you're not quite sure what you should do, then this is for you.

In this chart I am going to show you possible sources that will inspire you to come up with ideas for a debate. In some cases these will be things that you and your community care about. For others, it might be matters related to your work or industry or it could be proposed legislation that is already underway. So if you want to jump on somebody else's bandwagon that's fine. If you prefer to start with a blank page and figure it out on your own, that's OK too.

The one thing I want to mention is if you choose a source from the bottom row, the likelihood is that your idea or issue will be further along in the legislative process and may have a better chance of success. You'll also notice that compared to the top row, the bottom row is more specific. As you start drilling into an issue you will go from being a generalist with a vague idea about what the problem is to having a more specific and concrete point of view. I have excluded some sources you might think of because debate is about the issues, not about the candidates, elections or polling.

At the state level I have included California, Texas, New York and Florida sources. But every state has information related to their state legislation. So this is here just to act as a guideline for you and help get you started.

Sources for Debates and Issues

Your Community	The Media	Professional Association
• Local initiatives • Conversations with your neighbors • A problem you care deeply about that affects hundreds or thousands of people	• Local press • Your state capital press • Talk radio, NPR • National press – opinion, editorials (NYT, WSJ, IBD)	• Trade associations • Public policy think tanks • Special interest groups • Political committee policy platforms (RNC, DNC)
State Ballot Measures	**State Legislation**	**Federal Legislation**
• Ballotpedia • California Secretary of State	• California bills • California legislative analyst's office • Texas bills search • New York bills • Florida bill search	• Congress.gov • Congressional Research Service • Congressional Budget Office • Government Accountability Office • Office of Management and Budget • Office of Science and Technology Policy • OTA Archives

(* Web links are listed on the last page.)

Your first debate

On the "Start a Debate" page the first thing that you're going to do is start a debate and select a category. This drop-down should look familiar because it is the same 78 issue codes that you just looked at. Select the one that you think most appropriately represents the broad area you are focusing on for your issue.

Once you select the category, the page will fill in with its best guess at what House committee might first be looking at this particular bill. If your issue has to do with transportation it will bring up the Transportation committee. If it has to do with aviation, it may bring up the Committee on Science, Space and Technology.

In time, this will become more precise depending on if the issue is related to the federal, state or local level. But for the time being, if it is a federal issue the best guess will bring up only the federal members of Congress.

We will talk more about this later on.

Next, name your debate. You have a maximum of 42 characters here. Short simple statements are best. A title that suggests whether you are supporting or opposing something is stronger. And remember you are trying to convince people to support you. So for instance, "Blue Skies are Nice" is a much weaker title compared to "Support the Blue Sky Act H.R.1234."

This second title tells us three things that the first title does not. It tells us your position on the issue. i.e. you support it. It tells us what the specific Bill is, the Blue Sky Act. Finally it tells us that there is an existing bill in the House of Representatives and the number is H.R. 1234. This level of specificity gives more credibility to your debate.

If you want to find out if there is a bill related to the issue you are addressing, take a look at the links on the last page of the Debate Writer's Guide. Or glance at the chart above as it relates to state or federal legislation. You can search almost any issue by keyword, representative or Bill number. In most cases you will find that there are already bills in the legislature on the topic you were exploring.

Benefits of sponsored legislation

Is it important to align with an existing bill?

Well if your topic is already covered and somebody has already introduced a bill and it has sponsors or cosponsors, then the likelihood is that a lawmaker has given this some thought. If your idea closely matches to what they have drafted already, then it is in your best interest to support the existing legislation. By doing this you are ahead of the game. Sponsored legislation will give you a boost.

But if you want to create your own law or make a change to some existing law then you are free to put that in as you see fit. The disadvantage however, is that you do not yet have a sponsor or adoption of your idea and so in all likelihood it will take you longer to move your issue forward.

But it is your choice. You can go about it either way.

Most states, counties and cities will have links to pending legislation that you can locate in those jurisdictions as well.

So, you have filled in your category and named your debate. Now save it and move on to the next step.

The heavy lifting begins

Here you are going to describe what it is that you hope to accomplish.

The first field is where you present your argument. You can do this online at the site or if you prefer you can do it in a notepad or Microsoft Word and then refine it and copy in your text later on.

Funding and time

For our virtual funding we assume that you need a minimum of $5000 to move an issue forward. This is based on a very modest amount of what might be required to attract a small lobbying firm to your issue. Since this is virtual funding at this point, you are free to increase that number if you wish.

Your next choice is the number of days the debate should run for. If you think you will have a lot of immediate activity then you can select a shorter timeframe. But if you think that people need time to discover your debate, digest its content and make an informed decision as you build up your grassroots coalition, then a longer time period is recommended.

We have set the default to 180 days or six months. However you can choose to go either way or leave it as it is.

Debate statement

The next step requires a short debate statement. We have filled in three generic ones that you may use or if you wish you can create your own, provided it is as short as the ones you see in front of you.

This short debate statement is the one that appears at the top of the debate card on the home page.

Impact

The impact box relates to who would benefit and who could be hurt. You want to think about who might benefit from this in a material or financial way. It's always good to include both sides of the issue. So look at this and include the actual cost to the government, community or state. It is a wise thing to do.

If you don't state the full impact then someone else will. Not presenting all the facts makes it less likely that your issue will move forward. So it's worth understanding the impact of what you are proposing.

Photos

Before we go down to the sources that support and oppose I want to talk a little bit about the images. Based on the category you chose, we have selected one image that is a default image that will come up automatically for your debate. It is based on the issue category you chose.

However, you are free to add up to two additional images. You can also re-order them. The top image is the one that will appear on the debate card. In your debate these images will cycle through and rotate. Make sure you own or have the right to include any images that you select. You can always use your own or find royalty-free images on the web.

A quick tip here.

I would like to offer this thought about a way to think about what images to include.

A debate is about two sides of an issue. There is the positive side and the negative side. There is a proponent and there is an opponent. If your image visually shows the benefit for the proponent, that could be useful. On the other hand, it could show the destructive results of avoiding the issue.

One other aspect to consider is the image of a victim. In a classic battle, we have the hero, the opponent and the victim. In many cases you will find the same three elements in the structure of a debate. Often the opponent is doing something bad to the victim and as the debate author, we are trying to encourage unwilling heroes to come in to help a cause.

If you spend a little time thinking about this you will be able to come up with some novel and convincing visuals. You can also compare and contrast the positive or negative side of an issue by showing that in one image. A classic example of this was the campaign that showed your brain on drugs as an egg in a frying pan. The message was simple, visual and compelling. Don't do drugs.

I just want to mention this so you know that you have the ability to add your own creativity to the debate.

Sources

There are two more areas that I want to talk about.

The first is that it's important to include some backup to what you are saying. For instance, if you were trying to convince your mother that there was an important issue you would probably supply her with some links to a magazine article or a YouTube video that was recorded by a specific authority or subject matter expert. In academic circles you might want to pull in a white paper or a research report from a think tank. There are lots of possibilities out there.

If you Google your topic area you will find dozens of relevant links to what you are proposing. But you're not trying to make a one-sided case here. And I think that's important to understand. I believe you become more convincing if you can present both sides of an argument or at least supply both supporting and opposing information. This allows your reader to see both sides, decipher it for him or herself and come to their own conclusions.

Often we are missing this neutral, independent, non-biased opportunity when we receive information from a group regarding a particular issue. They only give us their point of view and they ignore the opposition. They leave off any facts that might be contrary to what they are proposing. I think this is a mistake.

It is not your job to ram your thoughts down somebody else's throat and convince them that you are right. That is propaganda.

It is your job to educate, inform and persuade the reader that you have a worldview on this topic, you are well informed and your support naturally leads to the advocacy of what it is you are proposing. Remember, this is a *"Political Persuasion Platform."* It mimics the kinds of activities you would actually undergo if you were to meet with your lawmaker and convince him that your point of view is the correct one. He will ask for opposition research. And if you don't have it, you can be sure that he will get it from somebody else.

So why not be an open, honest and reliable source and provide both sides of an argument so that your reader can use the resources that you have already pulled together and in some cases build upon that.

That's what an intelligent voter does. The more you do this in your debates, the more reliable you'll become and the more you will be considered to be an expert in your area.

So, find web links that support you, then Google other sites that take the opposing point of view. And see if through this synthesis of conflicting information you can arrive at a mutually beneficial solution that nobody else has thought of yet.

I mentioned that iLobby is a debate platform. And this is true. But in order to have a debate you need to be aware of both sides. In order to engage in intelligent conversation, you need to share your point of view and support it with factual arguments.

You notice I haven't said anything here about ad hominem attacks. In a debate these are not helpful. When they occur, they remove the focus from the actual issue and direct it to the character of the messenger. You saw examples of this in the last series of Republican presidential debates in 2016 when the attacks among the candidates became juvenile and nasty. It turns into a case of "He said, she said." It causes the viewer or audience to doubt both parties and become even more confused because they don't know which side to believe.

So you can avoid all of this confusion by doing two things; don't engage in ad hominem attacks, and to the best of your ability present both sides of an argument.

And that's why we are giving you fields to include web links that support your position and oppose your position.

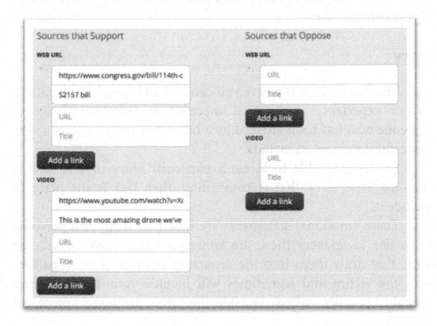

If you only show one side, the reader will know you are biased.

Finally, you can add multiple links by clicking on the blue Add a Link buttons.

Video

The links for adding video operate pretty much the same way. Try to find video links on YouTube that support both sides of your argument. Aside from the news channels or personal groups who put up videos you might also look at C-SPAN, which covers all government activity. If you include a YouTube link just make sure it is formatted correctly. You will be able to check this when you test your links a little bit later.

A new service available in California is <u>Digital Democracy</u>, which makes searchable legislative video available to the public at <u>https://digitaldemocracy.org.</u>

If you are an advocacy group or even an individual you can create your own video, post it to YouTube and then link it here to support your cause.

Story

This last section is where you can add additional information. In our experience, a personal anecdote or your knowledge of someone who has been affected by a bill either pro or con is a very powerful statement to include.

So if you're able to locate a particular story or you have a personal experience that is compelling, then this is the place to include it.

These emotional statements are based on truth and personal pain. For lawmakers these are sometimes the most convincing areas that draw them into the argument because they empathize with the victim and sometimes will include your story in their thought process when considering the proposed piece of legislation.

So if you have a personal story, include it. If you know someone who was harmed by a piece of legislation, include it. If you know of a case where a law in a community or district could easily be applied to another one, then include it.

Remember, your lawmaker does not have an unlimited attention span and infinite staff resources. So something you might think is insignificant could be the turning point for them. They don't have the time or energy to read every single argument from every single district and every magazine synopsis that comes their way. So what you think is insignificant might in fact be very important and something that they never thought of or saw.

About the author

This is you. If you have filled in your profile this is what will show up. Except for your ZIP Code. Instead, we will show your Congressional District, which is a much broader distribution of the population (about 700,000 constituents.)

Verification

Click the box that says that you are a registered US voter and then go ahead and enter the "CAPTCHA" phrase and click next.

Most of us are familiar with this verification method. It is used to stop robots and reduce spam.

If you get any errors then you will have to go back and correct those.

Edit or publish

Once you have completed this page, you will be taken to the next page and your debate will be in draft mode. The title in the box near the top will say "DEBATE PREVIEW - How your debate will look when it is published."

Warning

Don't vote on your own debate yet and don't pledge any money. Once you do, you will no longer be able to edit your debate.

Tip – Character count

If you used the Microsoft Word template we provided and wrote your debate up in Microsoft Word, then this is for you.

When you are done checking your character count and you're satisfied with the spelling and grammar and what you want to put into the debate on the website, you can copy and paste. I have one caveat however. Sometimes MS Word gives you an accurate character count including the spaces but when you try to paste it into our website it tells you that you have too many characters. This can occur because sometimes there are hidden characters that include fonts and formatting and they may exceed the character limit of what is allowed in each field.

If you find your debate is cut off after pasting it or if it simply does not fit, then here's what I would recommend. Either reduce the number of characters so it fits or paste it into a text only notepad first. If it is text only and the character count is accurate, you should not have a problem.

Review and test

Take a look at your debate and perhaps have someone review it to make sure that your thinking is rational and your spelling and grammar are satisfactory.

At this point you should also test your web and video links. If they are broken or do not work for some reason, then locate your original source and fix the links.

Remember, you want your debate to look as good as possible, and you want to be as convincing as possible. Go ahead and print a copy so that you can sit with it for a day or two and then when we come back we will move on to step seven.

Step 7 - Publish your debate

Well you've come a long way. You've gone through the six major steps and hopefully for you the first part was pretty easy.

You may have been challenged by step number six, creating a debate. But in the course of thinking through what needs to be included, I think you will find that presenting a concise argument to support a particular political position can be a bit challenging. And if you're honest with yourself, you will see that it takes a little more effort than simply painting a sign that says "No More War."

This is not about slogans. This is not about shouting. This is not about propaganda. This is not about special interests dominating the discussion.

This is about real people in their every day lives figuring out the issues that are important to them and putting together a one-page summary that will be compelling to leaders including lawmakers.

The more thoughtful, informed, and factual you are, then the greater the likelihood that you will be able to move your issue forward.

Professionals in public affairs, government affairs, and legislative staff perform this kind of thing every day. Perhaps not in this format but the routine is very similar. By completing this exercise in a disciplined and intelligent way, you are increasing the likelihood that you will attract a broad, sizable audience and that you will be taken seriously.

After all, isn't that what it's all about? Didn't you read this book so you could learn how to change a law? Well this is how it begins.

So I want to congratulate you for getting this far and honor your commitment to this process.

This is not an easy thing to do and perhaps that's why so few people actually do it.

You now have all the steps you need to create and publish a meaningful debate and begin to engage in the policy process. If you think about it, most of us only focus on the candidates for public office. We only vote every few years with the hope that the candidate that we voted for does their promised job.

Sometimes they do. Sometimes they don't. When they don't, we think our only recourse is to vote them out of office and elect somebody new. Well now you have a different tool in your hands, a tool you never had before.

After all when you think about it, you voted for someone because you thought that they would represent you and the issues that you and your community care about. Even if you did not have strong opinions about something, you probably felt that you had something to say or something to offer to the general discussion but there was no simple way to get the word out.

Well that has changed.

Now you have iLobby, a growing community of people who are concerned about our neighborhoods, our country and the world. People who would like to bring their point of view to the policy discussion – simply stated, have a real impact on their communities and the world.

So, I encourage you to go through the six steps and repeat them as many times as you like. If your issue gains traction and you get more people who are supporting your efforts, then eventually you will begin to build a reputable standing and a reliable coalition.

Eventually we will move onto the next stage of the service where you crowdfund your campaign. You will be able to hire a public affairs firm or a lobbying firm to help carry out your message through the halls of Congress or your state legislature.

That's what all the big companies do. And soon you can do it too.

Final thoughts

Some people have asked me if you can use iLobby at the state and local level. The answer is yes with an asterisk.

(*) The only difference is that your state assembly, Senate District or precinct number will not show up on our platform yet. Also we are not yet including your state and local lawmakers at this time. So you will not see the committees at the state level but that will come soon. Once there are enough people in the community using iLobby then this data will start to appear and become more relevant.

Eventually you will have a map of your political landscape by issue and the activity of the users on the site.

The other question that comes up has to do with matching you with the appropriate lobbyist to actually get a bill moved forward.

Generally, hiring a Washington lobbying firm is an expensive proposition. It usually requires a commitment of one year and at least $500,000-$1 million retainer to get something done. However there is a new breed of smaller shops in Washington and elsewhere that are willing to take on individual and small business clients at a more modest fee, about $5000 a month over a three month period.

We see this as a 10X - 25X reduction in cost which allows the smaller players to participate in the game.

In the 70s when Charles Schwab introduced the idea of affordable investing for individual investors, it was almost heresy to offer low cost trades. But what discount brokerage did was instead of shrinking the market, it actually expanded it. Previously, trading costs and fees were anathema for small investors. We see the same condition today with respect to lobbying and political access.

We also see crowdfunding as the solution to sharing the cost of hiring a lobbying firm. And this is what we are focusing on. So, if you have a debate and you are confident that you've gained momentum, built a large enough coalition, developed a clear mission and thus you know what you want to get done, then you might be concerned that you will be unable to raise the required funds until we remove the virtual currency constraint.

This is a little bit of a chicken and egg problem. If you have 100 people in your group and you've raised five dollars each, then you are not going to get the ear of a lobbying firm for $500. So remember my three principles: message, mass and money.

We help you with your message. But until you have a large mass of voters and you have real commitment and pledges, it's unlikely that we would be able to match you with a lobbyist just yet. But that is our primary goal.

As soon as we see that we have solved the chicken and egg problem and there is sufficient public interest to move issues and debates forward, at that time we will open it up to real funding and you will be able to hire a lobbying firm of your choice with the money that you have raised on our platform.

In the meantime, focus on your message and building your list of followers within your coalition.

Chapter 8

MOST COMMON MISTAKES

"The only thing necessary for the triumph of evil is for good men to do nothing."

~Edmund Burk~

Now that we have conquered how to do this, let me quickly outline what I think are the most common mistakes we make.

False beliefs

The <u>first</u> most common mistake we make is that we believe that we can't do anything. We know there are problems, but because we don't believe we can change them, we have given up. This false belief leads to inaction. We don't believe, we don't know, and we don't care. Our next mistake.

Apathy

The <u>second</u> and most common mistake that over 90% of the population makes is that we do nothing. We are not committed. We do not take the initiative. We do not care. This is not true for the top 1%. They are very politically active. The University of Chicago and Northwestern University put out a report about this in 2015, "*Democracy and The Policy Preferences of Wealthy Americans*". The top 1% don't always get what they want, but they often achieve more than what we are generally led to believe.

Ignorance

Finally the <u>third</u> most common mistake is that we are politically ignorant, misinformed and disinterested. This works against us, and leads us to frustration and ineffective actions. It's a self-fulfilling prophecy. We don't care. We don't know. We don't understand and therefore we don't connect. That's bad news all the way around.

On a more tactical level here are five additional mistakes we make.

Top Five Political Mistakes We All Make

1. We complain and blame

2. We don't talk to the right person
3. We employ fuzzy thinking
4. We focus on celebrity candidates, not real issues
5. We fail to build effective coalitions

If we get past these we often take ineffective action that isn't as durable as is required. (Top-five political mistakes <u>video</u>).

Chapter 9

TAKE ACTION NOW

"Take time to deliberate, but when the time for action has arrived, stop thinking and go."

~Napoleon~

Your 7-Step Challenge

Step 1 - (4 min.) Sign up at iLobby and vote on one debate.

Step 2 - (3 min.) Find a second debate and vote on it.

Step 3 - (10 min.) Add a short argument.

Step 4 - (9 min.) Pledge $50 of your virtual currency.

Step 5 - (3 min.) Share the debate on your favorite social media site.

Step 6 - (30 min.) Fill in your profile, read the quick start Debate Writer's Guide, then start a debate. Create the first draft of an issue you're passionate about. You don't have to publish it. Just save it. You can always come back later to make refinements.

Step 7 - (1 min.) Now publish your debate and tell the world what you think.

Total time required: 60 minutes

I want to congratulate you now that you have come this far.

By now you should realize that you could be part of the top 1% of the voter population. You now understand that issues are important, and policy matters. You know what you have to say matters. You believe that there are other people who believe in what you're doing and will support your point of view. And you know that someone has to take the initiative and make the first step.

Taking action always seems like a hard thing to do. But I have tried to break this down and make it very easy for you to start.

These are the seven key things you can do right now to get the ball rolling. These are simple steps. They require little effort, money or time.

But commitment is everything.

If you take these simple actions now and continue to do them again and again, then they will become habit. You can do Steps one through five on your mobile phone in minutes. Think of it, voting on issues anywhere, anytime.

By looking at your everyday environment, you will find problems and issues that concern you and you will become engaged. You will realize that you are able to make a difference. You will realize that you are not alone.

So for the time being relax and reflect. Pat yourself on the back. Congratulations! You did it. You are now a public policy expert.

You thought about an issue, voted on it, shared it with your neighbors and friends and made a simple but intelligent and perhaps even humorous comment that threw a compelling spotlight on your position. You helped someone else out with his or her debate.

That's really all there is to it. You don't need to be frightened by political issues. Getting into the game is easier than you think.

Changing the future is easier than you ever thought possible. And it might even be more fun and gratifying than you can imagine right now.

Thanks for staying with it.

Chapter 10

CONCLUSION

"The purpose of government is to enable the people of the nation to live in safety and happiness. Government exists for the interests of the governed, not for the governors."

~Thomas Jefferson ~

We've come a long way and I want to congratulate you again for sticking with it. You now know more than 99% of the population about how laws get made in the early stages. You're in a very small group.

Believe me, most people have no clue; which is unfortunate. Your responsibility now is to spread the word. Share the link so that others can download this book and get updates as we go along.

I think you can see now that the key factor is taking the initiative and committing to the process. You can also stay in touch with us by visiting our Facebook fan page (https://www.facebook.com/ ChangeALaw/) and reading comments from other people like you.

In 1984 anthropologist Margaret Mead said, *"Never doubt that a small group of thoughtful, committed citizens can change the world; indeed, it's the only thing that ever has."*

Well you are now in that small group of thoughtful, committed citizens. You can be very powerful. You can make change happen. You can improve your community, influence your leaders and impact the world.

But if you don't do anything—if you never commit, if you never stand up for what you believe in— nothing is going to change.

The world needs your help so you have to believe that the universe will support you. It's time to get to work and focus on the important things that matter in your life, your family, your community, and the world.

Think of yourself as an advocate. Persuade others to your point of view. Take the next step. Move your issue forward by changing a law.

I hope you'll join me in this effort. I hope you'll begin to realize and cherish the importance of your personal contribution. I hope you will stand up for democracy. When you get involved, you might find that you really enjoy it.

You won't regret this. With a single win, you'll be hooked to keep on doing great things for the people who matter, for strangers and for those who are less fortunate and cannot do it for themselves.

Thanks for taking the time to read this book and do the exercises.

Now, let's continue to...

Persuade simply, politely and eloquently.

BIBLIOGRAPHY

"'There Oughta Be a Law' Movement Lets Fed-up Citizens Write Their Own Laws." *The Christian Science Monitor*. The Christian Science Monitor. Web. 11 Nov. 2015.

21, April. "Sniper Fires at MCA High-Rise, Injures 7 : Violence: Police Identify the Gunman as a Former Employee of the Company. Two Secretaries on the 14th Floor Are Struck by Rounds." *Los Angeles Times*. Los Angeles Times, 21 Apr. 1993. Web. 11 Nov. 2015.

27, November. "Matsushita to Buy MCA--$6.5 Billion : Entertainment: The Deal for the Hollywood Conglomerate Is the Largest Takeover of a U.S. Company by a Japanese Firm. The Price Is Lower than Expected." *Los Angeles Times*. Los Angeles Times, 27 Nov. 1990. Web. 31 Jan. 2016.

28, May. "Attorneys Say Sniper Aimed at MCA's Image." *Los Angeles Times*. Los Angeles Times, 28 May 1993. Web. 11 Nov. 2015.

"3rd Annual There Ought to Be a Law Essay Contest -." *Rep. Tim Briggs*. Web. 11 Nov. 2015.

"Americans Legislative Exchange Council." Web. 11 Nov. 2015.

"Americans Name Government as No. 1 U.S. Problem." *Gallup.com*. Web. 18 Nov. 2015.

"Areas of Research." - *Congressional Research Service (Library of Congress)*. Web. 11 Nov. 2015.

"Arizona State University." – *Decision Theater Network*. Web. 12 Feb. 2016.

"Assemblywoman Starts 'There Ought to Be a Law' Contest." *Assemblywoman Starts 'There Ought to Be a Law' Contest*. Web. 11 Nov. 2015.

Baumgartner, Frank R. *Lobbying and Policy Change: Who Wins, Who Loses, and Why*. Chicago: U of Chicago, 2009. Print.

"The Best "Democracy" Money Can Buy: For Every Dollar Spent Influencing US Politics, Corporations Get $760 Back." Web. 11 Nov. 2015.

"Bills 'Sponsored' in Sacramento by Outside Groups Usually Become Law | Political Muscle | FaultLines | KQED News." *KQED News*. Web. 11 Nov. 2015.

Cialdini, Robert B. *Influence: The Psychology of Persuasion*. New York: Collins, 2007. Print.

"Congress and the Public." *Gallup.com*. Web. 18 Nov. 2015.

"Congress.gov | Library of Congress." *Congress.gov | Library of Congress*. Web. 11 Nov. 2015.

"Congressional Management Foundation | *Communicating with Congress*. Web. 11 Nov. 2015.

"Congressional Research Service Careers." *Congressional Research Service (Library of Congress)*. Web. 31 Jan. 2016.

"Crowdsourcing the Law." *Crowdsourcing the Law*. Web. 31 Jan. 2016.

DeKieffer, Donald E. *The Citizen's Guide to Lobbying Congress*. Chicago, IL: Chicago Review, 1997. Print.

Drutman, Lee. "CONGRESSIONAL FELLOWSHIP PROGRAM: The Complexities of Lobbying: Toward a Deeper Understanding of the Profession." *PS: Political Science & Politics APSC* 43.04 (2010): 834-37. Print.

Drutman, Lee. *The Business of America Is Lobbying: How Corporations Became Politicized and Politics Became More Corporate*. Print.

"EMPOWERING VOTERS." *ILobby*. Web. 11 Nov. 2015.

"Election Law Journal: Rules, Politics, and Policy." *The Seven Deadly Virtues of Lobbyists: What Lawyer Lobbyists Really Do*. Web. 31 Jan. 2016.

"Engaging Members in the Lobbying Process." *Association News*. Web. 11 Nov. 2015.

"Federal Taxes." *Tax Foundation*. Web. 31 Jan. 2016.

"Find Your California Representative." *Find Address*. Web. 11 Nov. 2015.

"Find Your Representative - Zip Code Lookup." *Find Your Representative - Zip Code Lookup*. Web. 13 Nov. 2015.

"Find Your Senators and Representatives." *- OpenCongress*. Web. 11 Nov. 2015.

Fitch, Bradford. *Citizen's Handbook to Influencing Elected Officials: Citizen Advocacy in State Legislatures and Congress*. Washington, D.C.: TheCapitol.Net, 2010. Print.

"Fixed Fortunes: Biggest Corporate Political Interests Spend Billions, Get Trillions." *Sunlight Foundation Blog*. Web. 11 Nov. 2015.

"Gamification of Politics for The Millennial Generation." *MILLENNIAL MAGAZINE RSS*. 04 Sept. 2015. Web. 11 Nov. 2015.

Gastil, John, and Peter Levine. *The Deliberative Democracy Handbook: Strategies for Effective Civic Engagement in the Twenty-first Century.* San Francisco: Jossey-Bass, 2005. Print.

"GovTrack.us." *GovTrack.us.* Web. 11 Nov. 2015.

"Greater Erie Assembly of Government Officials' "There Ought to Be a Law" Essay Contest Remarks :: May 7, 2015." *State Senator Sean Wiley.* Web. 11 Nov. 2015.

"Key Issues for Returning California Legislature." *Sacbee.* Web. 11 Nov. 2015.

Kush, Christopher. *The One-hour Activist: The 15 Most Powerful Actions You Can Take to Fight for the Issues and Candidates You Care about.* San Francisco: Jossey-Bass, 2004. Print.

Leech, Beth L. *Lobbyists at Work.* Print.

"Legislative Action: Working Together to Influence Public Policy." *LWV.* Web. 11 Nov. 2015.

"Legislative Analyst's Office." *Legislative Analyst's Office.* Web. 13 Nov. 2015.

"Lobbying Advice for Business Owners." *Resources for Entrepreneurs at Gaebler Ventures RSS.* Web. 11 Nov. 2015.

"Lobbying Database." *Opensecrets RSS.* Web. 11 Nov. 2015.

"The Lobbying Strategy Handbook." *Google Books.* Web. 11 Nov. 2015.

"Lobbying Targets." *Strategic Influence in Legislative Lobbying.* Print.

Lofgren, Mike. *The Party Is Over: How Republicans Went Crazy, Democrats Became Useless, and the Middle Class Got Shafted.* Print.

"Lorelei Kelly | How to Give Congress Back Its Brain(s) | PDF13 HD." *YouTube.* YouTube. Web. 05 Mar. 2016.

"Major Donors Consider Funding Black Lives Matter." *POLITICO.* Web. 18 Nov. 2015.

Mann, Thomas E., and Norman J. Ornstein. *It's Even Worse than It Looks: How the American Constitutional System Collided with the New Politics of Extremism.* New York: Basic, 2013. Print.

Mann, Thomas E., and Norman J. Ornstein. *The Broken Branch: How Congress Is failing America and How to Get It Back on Track.* Oxford: Oxford UP, 2006. Print.

Mobile Reference. *Politics by Aristotle.* Boston: MobileReference.com, 2008. Print.

Mordecai, Adam. "A Guy Does Some Simple Math To Explain Why Saying 'My Vote Doesn't Matter' Is Actually A Bad Idea." Web. 13 Nov. 2015.

"NACo." *NACo*. Web. 11 Nov. 2015.

"New America." *New America*. Web. 05 Mar. 2016.

"News - Legislative Analysis, Bulletins." *Republican Study Committee*. Web. 07 Mar. 2016.

Newsom, Gavin Christopher, and Lisa Dickey. *Citizenville: How to Take the Town Square Digital and Reinvent Government*. Print.

"Nick Allard on the Reputation of Lobbying." *YouTube*. YouTube. Web. 31 Jan. 2016.

"PA State Rep. Thomas Murt - Murt Announces Winners in 'There Ought to Be a Law' Contest." *PA State Rep. Thomas Murt - Murt Announces Winners in 'There Ought to Be a Law' Contest*. Web. 11 Nov. 2015.

Phillips, Kevin. *The Politics of Rich and Poor: Wealth and the American Electorate in the Reagan Aftermath*. New York: Random House, 1990. Print.

"Political Advocacy Can Help Your Business | 8020 Blog." Web. 11 Nov. 2015.

"Political Party Time." *Sunlight Foundation's Party Time*. Web. 11 Nov. 2015.

"RealClearPolitics - Election Other - Congressional Job Approval." *RealClearPolitics - Election Other - Congressional Job Approval*. Web. 18 Nov. 2015.

"RealClearPolitics - Election Other - Direction of Country." Web. 18 Nov. 2015.

"Recent Updates." *Congressional Management Foundation*. Web. 31 Jan. 2016.

Reich, Robert B. *Saving Capitalism: For the Many, Not the Few*. Print.

"Rep. Aument's Legislative Report: There Ought to Be a Law Contest Winner." *YouTube*. YouTube. Web. 11 Nov. 2015.

"Report Exposes 8 Ways the Super Rich Want to Control American Politics — and It's Very Bad News for the Rest of Us." *Raw Story*. Web. 31 Jan. 2016.

"Senator Jerry Hill Announces." *Senator Jerry Hill*. Web. 11 Nov. 2015.

"The Size of State Legislatures." *Economix The Size of State Legislatures Comments*. 31 Dec. 2013. Web. 12 Nov. 2015.

"There Oughta Be a Law!" *Senator Anthony H Williams.* Web. 11 Nov. 2015.

"The U.S Spends $5.9 Billion on Foreign Military Financing." *HowMuch.* Web. 11 Nov. 2015.

"U.S. Government Accountability Office (U.S. GAO)." *U.S. Government Accountability Office (U.S. GAO).* Web. 31 Jan. 2016.

"The United States Conference of Mayors - Usmayors.org." *The United States Conference of Mayors - Usmayors.org.* Web. 11 Nov. 2015.

Turpen, Elizabeth and Kelly, Lorelei. *Policy Matters: Educating Congress on Peace and Security.* Washington, D.C.: Henry L. Stimson Center, 2004. Print.

Vance, Stephanie D. *Citizens in Action: A Guide to Influencing Government.* Bethesda, MD: Columbia & Information Services, 2009. Print.

Vogel, Kenneth P. *Big Money: 2.5 Billion Dollars, One Suspicious Vehicle, and a Pimp-on the Trail of the Ultra-rich Hijacking American Politics.* Print.

"When Lobbyists Literally Write The Bill." *NPR.* NPR. Web. 31 Jan. 2016.

Will, George F. "Opinions." *Washington Post.* The Washington Post. Web. 11 Nov. 2015.

"Welcome." *California Legislative Information.* Web. 13 Nov. 2015

TESTIMONIALS

> *"Man is by nature a political animal."*
> ~**Aristotle**~

This is for any American who believes they can change the system. Great idea! Lobbying is more effective than protesting or signing petitions. Protesting is totally co-opted by the very people they're supposed to be protesting against.

- Jackie T. (WA-07) Constituent # 373605B

As a young adult I feel that our generation does not matter to the government whatsoever. At least this is some way to voice an opinion that might actually be heard.

- Mike K. (WI-03)

The site is very intriguing as it seems a more cost-effective way to ensure the voice of the small business owner is heard. I really like the concept.

- John G. (IL-10) Constituent # 363256A

I think this site is a really good idea. I think this site is definitely made to benefit the silent majority. Many of them could benefit from it too. I imagine that there must be a way to make or start a debate, vote on it and then send a copy of the results to your state representative. This would be one way that users can actually feel like they are making a difference and their opinions matter.

- Cameron L. (NY-20)

I liked creating my own debate and then having others be able to vote on it. I never thought about hiring my own lobbyist. I wasn't even aware I could do that. So I like that too. I guess I would be willing to pay maybe $25-$50 a week if I knew he or she could actually make some real change. I think anybody who has any positive ideas for change could use this site.

- Betty R. (PA-15)

Small business owners would be the best users. They can probably benefit more from direct change on bills. Lobbying is more effective than protesting or signing petitions... definitely. Lobbying means money and nothing moves in Washington without money.

- Rachel E. (TX-06) Constituent # 376717B

I believed it was a rich man's' game. $5 a month would seem reasonable if it was effective.

- Brian S. (FL-07) Constituent # 363256C

I would be willing to pay $100/month. I like the idea of crowdsourcing issues and presenting them like a lobbyist.

- George R. (CA-08) Constituent # 363256B

My neighbors would use this site. I don't think $25 is too much to ask especially if others are willing to make the same contribution. I would. I think lobbying is more effective than protesting or signing petitions. Although I think lobbying should be illegal, we have to start somewhere.

- Tom S. (CA-30) Constituent # 373605C

I would be willing to pay a fee for the chance to really change a law because money is used to persuade.

- Jane K. (NC-09) Constituent # 373605D

Lobbying is often extremely effective and is usually more effective than protesting or signing petitions.

- Patrick H. (AR-04) Constituent # 373605E

I love this concept. The interaction and the ability to create our own issues and debates are great. This is what people have been looking for... a voice. The ability to track, share, debate and educate on issues and the needs of our country is really awesome.

- Jill B. (OR-02) Constituent # 1154898A

How much would my neighbor contribute to a cause that meant something to them? It really depends on the cause. If I felt it would make a difference... $2500. This is for folks like me. People who are active voters and look for ways to stay informed on issues and participate in politics. I think it is more effective than signing petitions.

- Rob G. (SC-04) Constituent # 376717A

I can put my point of view out there without any questions. I think this is a great site for people to discuss concerns.
- Adam S. (FL-08) Constituent # 363256C

I feel that people talk about making change all of the time. We don't know how to bring about change because it seems like it's too much work, too much time, and we wouldn't know who to contact. iLobby eliminates all of those issues. That video about how iLobby works does a very good job of explaining how you can get help with bringing about change.
- Jackson K. Constituent # 839271B

I love the idea and the brash self-confidence with which it is put before us! The challenge now is to bridge the process of constructing these bridges between self-initiative and government action.
- Asher F. Constituent # 839271A

If a lobbyist had a remote chance of striking down this corruption I would pay upwards of $500 to really have our voices heard (assuming it was a big movement not just 10 or 20 people). This should be marketed to social media sites and get people to voice their opinions and communicate with others in an organized and healthy manner.
- Patrick H. (AR-04) Constituent # 373605E

I would pay for a lobbyist if I felt strongly about my cause... I think anyone with a specific political agenda/cause would enjoy the comparison feature to get an understanding of their elected officials' positions.
- Chris J. (FL-07)

It looks like a good platform to further my cause and get people and resources behind the idea.
- Dori B. Constituent # 839271C

The debate section was really quite enjoyable. It seems like it might make a good forum for discussion although whether that would translate into lobbying dollars remains to be seen. I find the idea that I have to lobby my (sic) elected representatives a bit distasteful but I understand the realities of marketing a position. I might consider hiring a lobbyist if I had a large economic stake in an issue and if that were the case I may pledge several hundred dollars if it appeared to be a wise investment.

- * User P1 Constituent # 1484516A

I am a small business. I like the empowerment of each individual to believe his or her voice is heard. It's a great way to get people aware of other ideas and possibilities that are out there in cyberspace that might have clout.

- Barry S. (FL-08) Constituent # 363256C

As a small business owner where costs are high it's a challenge to justify this type of expenditure when I feel my chances of success are so low. So this iLobby site was very intriguing as it seemed a more cost-effective way to ensure the voice of the small business owner is heard. Overall solid site, I really like the concept.

- John H. (IL-09) Constituent # 363256A

I like that it simplifies the process of having laws changed. All you have to do is start it or participate and the rest is easy. The idea of getting together with support(ers) and a little bit of $$ and change the law is great. It gives average people a platform to be able to get the things that they want passed.

- Asher F. Constituent # 839271A

People love to express themselves and if given a political environment they would do so with passion, in my opinion. The best user would be someone who is passionate about the issues they believe in and want to influence others and ultimately Congress. Lobbying is more effective because yes obviously, they've managed to place into the public mind that the protesters are freeloaders.

- Leonora H. (CA-04) Constituent # 373605A

I loved that it enables people to kickstart political issues that are important to them/me and take issues into their own hands all from their computer. It is an excellent tool for independents and people that really want to push a public bill in the 'right' direction and help it pass the legislature.

- Dan F. (WA-07) Constituent # 1484516C

It's a very interesting concept. The debate aspect is different than other places.

- Mark D. (KY-06) Constituent # 1484516D

In an election year there are plenty of opinions out there and the need to make your voice heard is multiplied. Petitions may get something on the ballot but they rarely pass whatever the issue is. Lobbying is effective because I think it unites like a petition. It also raises capital to further your agenda, which protesting and petitions cannot do.

- Leonora H. (CA-04) Constituent # 373605A

I love this concept. The interaction and the ability to create our own issues and debates is great. This is what people have been looking for...a voice. The ability to track, share, debate and educate on issues and the needs of our country is really awesome.

- Jan T. Constituent # 1154898A

It was easy to use, fun to read and let me know some good bills coming up and trying to get promoted. Something I have a hard time keeping up with! I think Americans get very confused with the system and think their opinion doesn't matter because it doesn't change anything. Maybe a good example of a bill that they might care about depending on their demographics or a quick survey about them would help.

- * Larry A. Constituent # 1483760A

The best user would be someone who is passionate about the issues they believe in and want to influence others and ultimately Congress.

- Lauran L. (CA-04) Constituent # 373605A

I like that it was an easy way for people to become more involved in issues.

- Summer J. (MN-01) Constituent # 1154898B

I like that it's an attempt to grab the new generation for politics, both local and national.

- * Charles B. Constituent # 1483760B

I would (use it.) I'm very active in local politics and find this site intriguing and compelling. Please let me know when it is out of beta. I would like to spread the word.

- Tom S. (CA-30) Constituent # 373605C

Note: These testimonials are from early iLobby users and testers. Beta testers were paid for testing but not for their comments. They were free to say anything they want. Where indicated (*) some users signed in pseudonymously with a username we provided, "CitizenOne". So, no congressional district was available. A few comments were edited for brevity and clarity.

ABOUT ILOBBY

We bring a scarce and expensive resource for policy change to the average American voter. iLobby is a crowd funded lobbying platform. We help voters engage in public policy so you can get laws passed to improve your community, influence your leaders and impact the world.

The average American voter has no real political power. We generally use ineffective tactics to change policy, which leads to mixed and often disastrous results. iLobby's mission is to take what the top 1% does very effectively and make it available to the remaining 99% of frustrated voters in this country. We empower voters to change laws because we need now more than ever, the combined intelligence and commitment of American voters to solve some of the world's greatest challenges.

We believe in the dignity and voice of the voter.

At iLobby our driving mission is to empower you to change laws so that you can have an impact on your community and the world.

We believe in the wisdom of the crowd.

We are nonpartisan, independent and issue agnostic. We believe that if you are well informed ahead of time, then you can make up your own mind about an issue. We believe the best way to do this is through open and honest debate. We are voter centric. We respect the individual voter.

We want to empower you to have the information and the tools you need to affect change simply and conveniently.

Sometimes this means passing a new law. Other times it means preventing bad policy from becoming law. To do this we need to work with and educate our leaders and legislators. We don't tell them what to do. You do. We don't tell you how to think. You do. We know you can think for yourself. We do not need to be told that there is only one point of view when we know there are many.

Too often we know there are problems that we face and usually the solution is a policy or legislative decision. Sometimes individual groups amass great power and control the decisions for the rest of us. But for many working parents it's difficult to attend the town hall meeting or write a well-thought-out letter to a newspaper or your congressman. It's difficult to wait on hold for an hour on the phone while you wait to get your two minutes of fame on talk radio.

We know voters are angry and frustrated. But we think it is important for voters to abandon non-productive actions and instead engage with lawmakers, early and often. To that end we have dedicated ourselves to building an efficient Townhall format coupled with a lobbyist matching system so voters can have access to professional lobbying firms. We are not saying that this is a silver bullet and will always succeed. What we are saying is that at least it will give you more options than you have now.

Too often people think, "It's the law and there's nothing you can do about it." Well that's just not true. There is something you can do. You can change the law. You can amend a law, you can repeal a law or you can propose a new law. You don't have to wait for someone else to do it. You can do it and you can do it now.

We want to level the playing field and give you a fighting chance. We believe voters are smart and have common sense answers to problems. We want to encourage dialogue between voters and your representatives so that you can make positive change for everyone.

ABOUT THE AUTHOR

John Thibault is the founder and CEO of **iLobby**. He previously served in government affairs at MCA/Universal. John was also the first VP of business development and marketing at eBay and the first VP of marketing at Financial Engines. He holds a Bachelor's degree from Ryerson University and an MFA from UCLA. He has been published in several magazines including Association News, Manufacturing Today, CEO for High Growth Ventures and Millennial Magazine. He enjoys skiing and more recently fly boarding and lives with his wife and three children in Northern California. He can be reached at john@ilobby.co

BONUS

Bonus #1

If you got this far and jumped in and did the seven steps, then you may want to get more specific information about how it all fits together. So I am offering this free online video training mini-course that will help get you started. Just sign up at Change a Law Minicourse. http://bit.ly/28MQ0qW

In this *"free"* training you will learn:

- How to become an advocate for a cause you really believe in.
- The 3 essential components every policy campaign must have.
- The 5 critical mistakes most people make.
- The 7 key steps to advocacy success.
- Why issue clarity is essential for you to move ahead.
- How to turn awareness into action.
- Tactical advice that anyone can follow.
- Identify how to influence public policy and get the laws you really want using iLobby.
- Focus on issues and never be frustrated with politics again.
- More than 60 minutes of simple, tactical advice that anyone can follow.

Bonus #2

Download our free Debate Writer's Guide (https://www.ilobby.co/sites/default/files/ilobby-co-debate-writers-guide.pdf). This will give you a quick overview of how the debate will look.

If you have stories, comments, thoughts or feedback about this book please feel free to contact us at feedback@changealaw.com

Or visit Facebook http://www.facebook.com/ChangeALaw

For the truly daring who want to change a law, visit
https://www.ilobby.co   Sign up for our newsletter and start your
own debate.

Links Mentioned In This Book

https://www.ilobby.co
https://www.ilobby.co/debate/support-hr3669-safe-drone-act-2015
https://www.facebook.com/ChangeALaw/
http://www.changealaw.com/minicourse
http://www.house.gov/representatives/find/
https://lda.congress.gov/LD/help/default.htm?turl=Documents%2F
AppCodes.htm
https://www.ilobby.co/sites/default/files/ilobby-co-debate-writers-
guide.pdf
http://www.senatorsimitian.com/oughta/
https://www.youtube.com/watch?v=MPdzwfZTGOU
https://digitaldemocracy.org
https://www.youtube.com/watch?v=EhQmsKeT1bg

Sources for Debates and Issues

https://ballotpedia.org/Public_policy_in_California
http://www.sos.ca.gov/elections/ballot-measures/qualified-ballot-
measures/
https://leginfo.legislature.ca.gov/faces/billSearchClient.xhtml
http://www.lao.ca.gov
http://www.capitol.state.tx.us/Search/TextSearch.aspx
http://assembly.state.ny.us/leg/
https://legiscan.com/FL
https://www.congress.gov
https://www.loc.gov/crsinfo/research/
https://www.cbo.gov
http://www.gao.gov/key_issues/overview
https://www.whitehouse.gov/omb
https://www.whitehouse.gov/administration/eop/ostp
https://www.princeton.edu/~ota/

CPSIA information can be obtained
at www.ICGtesting.com
Printed in the USA
LVOW05s0410290817

546688LV00007B/96/P

9 780692 676707